The important thing is not to stop questioning.
(Attributed to Albert Einstein)

My heart cannot rejoice in what my mind rejects.
(Variously attributed)

Truth does not fear investigation.
(Common Christian saying)

In from the Rain

A Journey of Faith

Brett Christensen

Unless otherwise indicated, scripture quotations in this work are from the English Majority Text Version of the Holy Bible, New Testament (EMTV). ©2002-2003 Paul W. Esposito

Paperback published by Brett Christensen.
ISBN 978-0-9942441-1-6

Order enquiries:
servantofChrist0@gmail.com
or through most book retailers.

National Library of Australia Cataloguing-in-Publication entry
Creator: Christensen, Brett N., 1963- author.
Title: In from the Rain: a Journey of Faith
ISBN: 978-0-9942441-1-6
Subjects: Christensen, Brett N., 1963-
             Faith and reason—Christianity.
             Belief and doubt.
Dewey number: 234.23

Foreword

This is the story of my search for New Testament Christianity. While the account is accurate (to the best of my recollection), most names have been changed for the sake of the privacy of the individuals involved.

Over the years I have noticed heightened interest when I talk about where I've come from and the circumstances of my conversion. My wife Lesley has urged me many times to put my story into print, being convinced that it would help others. If it does help anyone, it will have been worth the time writing it down. I pray that it helps and blesses you.

Mega-thanks to Lesley, Dale, Kim, Bryce, Greg McPherson and the Poyntons for offering feedback and pointing out typos. Much thanks to all who, knowingly or otherwise, helped me in my journey of faith thus far, the biggest thanks of course going to the Lord God who masterminded it all and continues his work to bring it to its ultimate fruition.

Brett Christensen, March 2015

"I Stand at the Door and Knock"

"I've been praying to meet someone like you." That has to be one of the nicest compliments anyone has paid me. What do you say to a comment like that?

I had opened the front door to find two young men standing there, faces I didn't recognise. They weren't wearing suits, so I immediately gathered they were not Mormons or JWs. Saturday morning seemed to be the favourite time for JWs to come knocking and, whether JW or Mormon, they always seem to pick a time that I'm tied up doing something. But I always do my best to speak to them, because they have taken time out of their own lives to come to my door to talk about God.

If you come to my door wanting to talk about God, you've picked the right door. I love talking about God. If I can, I'll invite you in and open the scriptures with you to see whether the things you're saying are so.[1] Nothing I'm doing is more important than doing that, so the painting or lawn-mowing or dishes can wait. Especially the dishes.

I've spent hours reasoning from the scriptures[2] with Mormons and JWs, having them back for further discussions. There are so few people around who care enough about spiritual matters to even open a Bible, that when I come across someone who wants to do it — and they even take the effort to come to my door — then I'm going to do my best to give them my time and attention.

But these two young men didn't have suits on or black leather briefcases with them, so I figured they must have been selling something. To my pleasant surprise, they did want to talk about spiritual things. They offered me a tract, "How You Can Be Sure You're Going to Heaven", and talked about it. It turns out they were Baptists. This was a first for me: I'd never before had a Baptist come knocking on my door. And these ones were from a church about

---

[1] Acts 17:11

[2] Acts 17:2

half an hour's drive from my neighbourhood, so they had indeed come a long way for a chat.

While we were talking, I had a quick look through the tract they had given me, and I saw that it taught something which I used to accept, but which I'd later learned was quite different to the message the apostles of Christ went out preaching at his command. Perhaps they didn't realise this, just as I hadn't realised it years ago until someone explained the way of God more accurately to me.[3] I invited Tran and Greg in.

"Do you ever see the apostles or other disciples in the book of Acts telling people what this tract is telling people about how to be saved and go to heaven?" I asked them.

They admitted that they had not.

"No, me neither. In Acts I see them again and again telling people how to be saved, the same way for everyone, and it's very different to what this tract says. Do you remember what Paul said in Galatians 1 about anyone preaching a different gospel message to what he preached?"

I roughly quoted what Paul said in Galatians 1:7-8 and they seemed to remember the passage.

"So it's pretty serious stuff, isn't it, to be telling people something different to what Paul told people?"

They agreed. I certainly didn't want them to be handing out material to people in my (or any) neighbourhood which would mislead people by telling them "a different gospel". And, thinking about what Paul says about this, I also didn't want these two sincere young men to be doing something for which they would be "accursed".

We stood just inside my front door as we spoke more about these things, and it was there that Tran dropped his compliment. I know

---

[3] Acts 18:26

he was just telling me what was true, but I took it as a compliment. I don't know how awkward I sounded as I responded, but I said something to the effect that it's nice to be the answer to his prayer!

Despite his compliment, I couldn't persuade them to come sit in the loungeroom and open the scriptures together. Greg was not so pleased to have met me, and said they would need to talk to their Pastor about the things I was saying. He wanted to leave. So I said, "Well, you know where to find me, so if you do want to talk about this more, I'll be happy to." I wrote my name and phone number on a piece of paper, and handed it to Tran.

I never saw or heard from them again.

Our family certainly prayed for them. I could relate to Tran, a young man with a zeal for God, to the degree that he would knock on the doors of strangers to talk about God. I actually did that when I was still in high school. I didn't pray to meet someone who could explain the way of God more accurately to me. I didn't think I needed it. But God knew I needed it, and he arranged it for me anyway. But he had to get me to the stage that I would listen, and he started working on that years before I met Jeff.

Small Steps

I grew up in Aspendale, a bayside suburb of Melbourne. There were lots of good things about my childhood, but the best thing was that I was given an awareness of God. I don't remember my parents talking much about him, but we were a church-going family, and on Sundays somebody would "say grace" at the dining room table before our family ate lunch. I remember being asked to say it at least once: "For what we are about to receive, Lord make us truly thankful. For Christ's sake the Lord, amen." I was young enough to be excused for not saying it word-perfect. I didn't really understand it all, but I got the broad idea.

Sometime in my early childhood, we stopped "saying grace", but we kept going to church most Sundays. There were two churches in our suburb: around the corner from our house was the Catholic Church, with "the Catholic School"; up on Station Street was the Presbyterian Church, the one we would walk to. It only took five minutes. As I recall it, the chapel proper was not very large — an unobtrusive cream brick building, lower than street level, with a larger, older-looking "Sunday School hall" attached to the back. Trains would rumble past on the high side of Station Street every 40 minutes or so.

Sunday School was after church. My parents would go home, and my brother, sister and I would stay on for Sunday School. My brother was five years older than me — he still is, strangely enough — so afterwards I was safely escorted home with my sister (three years older), where *World of Sport* was on the telly while the Sunday roast was being prepared. Football was more the religion of our household than anything else. This was typical of Melbourne families in the late 1960s and early 70s, the era of my childhood.

But being in a church-going family, I did get a concept of God, and I would have casual conversations with him when I was very young. Perhaps "conversation" isn't the right word, since I did all the talking. But I knew he was up there listening; that's what I had been told, probably at Sunday School.

I only remember my mother telling me this once. I was alone in my room one night, and for some reason I had a go at praying. I knelt by the bed and put my face into my hands. I was not in the habit of doing this, so I don't know why I did it on this occasion. Perhaps I was already kneeling for something else I was doing, or perhaps I got the concept from a song my father sang to me when I was younger, from A.A. Milne's poem:

> *Little boy kneels at the foot of his bed*
> *Droops on little hands little gold head*
> *Hush, hush, whisper who dares?*
> *Christopher Robin is saying his prayers*[4]

I wasn't at the foot of my bed; just the side. My brother and I shared a room, but he wasn't there. Our beds, covered with orange bedspreads, were against opposite walls, and there was enough room between them for a chest of drawers against the window, next to our bedheads. The view from our window, when it was light, was of our side fence and the Taylors' house next door.

Kneeling beside my bed, I started by asking God to show me that he is listening. (Was this the early skeptic in me?) Immediately the dog next door, normally a quiet dog, barked vehemently. I was so excited by this, I ran out to the kitchen and told my mother what had just happened when I asked God to show me that he was listening.

"Oh, he's always listening," she assured me without stopping what she was doing.

In all my excitement, I don't think I got around to saying anything else in my prayer. But it was a moment that stuck with me, a small but significant step in my journey. I was convinced that God was listening, and I was happy to keep talking to him. It would be years before I learned to listen to him.

---

[4] A A Milne, 'Vespers' in *When We Were Very Young*, Methuen & Co., London, 1924

I have wondered what would have happened if that dog did not bark so uncharacteristically. I can only guess, because that's not what happened. Whether it was God's doing or not, God certainly used that moment for good in my life. Bad things happened to me in my childhood, too, and in retrospect I can see that God also used those things for good, even though they were not his doing.

Another good thing which stands out as a milestone for me was in 1978, when I was in my fourth year of high school. It was an uncomfortable moment for me, and probably insignificant to the person God used to prod me. I was at "Mordi High School" (which is what we called Mordialloc-Chelsea High School for short). Luke Franzi was sitting next to me in class and he asked if I was coming to something at church that weekend. His family were devout members of the congregation. They probably wouldn't be comfortable with that description, but from my point of view they were an example of what it was to be full-on committed church members.

Luke was a kind and encouraging friend, an enthusiastic participant in church activities, and without his friendship, who knows which way I would've gone. Yes, God knows. When Luke asked whether I was going to be at something the youth were doing that weekend, and I said I probably wouldn't be, Luke replied, "Too busy for God."

It may have been just an observation he was making, or he may have been saying it to gently prod my conscience. It certainly worked. There were other things I wanted to do. Like the rest of my family, I wasn't one to attend church every Sunday, or youth meetings. I went if I felt like it, and often that depended on how much I wanted to get away from my family at the time.

Luke's words sank in and I didn't reply. I don't know whether I ended up going to whatever was happening that weekend, but I do know that Luke's comment created a turning point in my thinking. I could see he had summed me up pretty well. God wasn't number one in my life. I was in the habit of just being the occasional church-goer, when there was nothing more appealing on offer. That put me in pole position to start down the road of fading interest in God. His words pulled me up and made me rethink my priorities. This time it wasn't a dog God was using, but one of my friends — a true friend, who cared enough to say four words that made me uncomfortable. I did care about God, and I didn't want to ever be too busy for him.

It won't surprise you that I soon started going along to youth group every time I could. The youth group leaders were seven or eight lovely people, sincere and enthusiastic, and the oldest of them was 25. They really did care about us and I really responded to that. I felt loved. They ran great Friday nights and camps as well. Some of them also ran the Sunday morning Youth Bible Class. In hindsight I can see their love and sincerity did not compensate for their lack of knowledge of the scriptures, but they certainly knew more Bible than I did, and without the love they showed, I would not have been drawn into their influence. These were some more people I am sure God used in his ongoing work to draw me nearer to him. One of them, a girl four years older than me, encouraged me significantly a couple of years later, but I'll tell you about that soon enough.

A Leap Year

The middle of 1978 was a dreamtime for me. We had lived in New York for three years, and now I was back in my home town, Aspendale, going to the footy and listening to Australian music I had missed so much.

In the space of six months that year, during which I turned 15, I developed a keen enthusiasm for God and Christianity (helped by Luke's friendship). People at the Presbyterian Church could see it, and told me so. My parents could also see it, and I think it worried them. Somewhere in the dead of winter I came home from a Sunday night meeting at church where they'd had a guest speaker talking to us about the signs that a "one world government" was coming soon, one which would control our economy so much that we could not buy or sell without its approval. He told us this was in fulfilment of predictions made in the book of Revelation, so it was something to be excited about and to make sure we stuck with God, rather than give any allegiance to the coming Beast.

When I got home I stood by the open fire in our loungeroom and told my parents about what this man had been saying. To my disappointment, they questioned his claims, and warned me about crackpots who claimed all sorts of weird things — conspiracy theories and doomsday predictions. My father, a Collins Street banker (a Wall Street banker for three years), pointed out some things which threw water on my excitement about what I had heard that night. In short, his point was *don't believe everything you hear* — a very important lesson parents have to teach their naïve youngsters. I remember, when I was much younger, coming into the house with some junk mail from our letterbox and excitedly telling my parents about an offer of lots of money. I couldn't understand why they didn't share my excitement. "People don't give you something for nothing," was my father's pronouncement. It was a sad lesson to receive, but one every parent has to give their children. (It turns out it's not entirely true, either. God is the big exception to that rule, and his people follow suit in varying degrees.)

During the winter of 1978, one of the youth group leaders gave me a book which her mother had given her to pass on. The book was titled "A Time for Decision". I felt just a little offended by this, because as far as I was concerned I'd already made a decision to be a Christian. At youth group I joined singing "I Have Decided to Follow Jesus" and meant every word of it. *No turning back, no turning back.* Nobody sat me down to teach me how to become a Christian. It just became apparent if you were a believer. Plus of course you started saying that you were. What you said and what you did showed to the people around you that you believed in Jesus. By the time I was handed this book, people could see where my allegiance was. Strangely enough, I think this is why this youth group leader's mother gave her the book to give to me.

My mother seemed to take exception to it as well. "You've already made your decision." She was referring to my confirmation. The Presbyterian Church's official line on how to become a Christian was to be christened (which they also called being baptised), and your parents could do that to you as a baby. Confirmation was merely a ceremony to declare that you confirm the choice your parents made on your behalf. The obvious question is: Why not leave the christening until I was old enough to make that decision for myself? Well, you see, our church's doctrine was that even as a baby I needed to be saved from eternal damnation. I was born guilty, they held, not because I had sinned, but because Adam sinned. So I was doomed to be damned for someone else's sin. This wasn't explained to ordinary church members (unless you pinned the minister down for an explanation), but that's what lay behind the practice of "christening" and "confirmation".[5]

But we "lay members" had the idea that you just became a Christian by osmosis. Faith grew, and it showed. Being confirmed (or christened, if you hadn't had it done as a baby) was seen more as the way to become a member of the church. By doing it, you declared your affiliation with the Presbyterian Church. I did that in 1977 (when I lived overseas), and I was genuine about it, but it wasn't until 1978, back home in Aspendale, that I started to take my commitment to God seriously.

---

[5] This was a doctrine the Presbyterians had inherited from the Catholics, centuries ago.

Around this time, Luke loaned me a book which was along the same lines as that American visiting speaker's message. It was called *The Late Great Planet Earth*, by Hal Lindsey. I don't know how many people had read it, but this copy looked like it had been handed around plenty. It spoke about current events as being part of the fulfilment of prophecies in the Bible, and by the time I got my hands on it the claims were already eight years old. Hal Lindsey pointed to events in the world which he said were signs that the end of the world was nearing, and he said that believers in Jesus would be taken to heaven before things got really bad – an event popularly called "the rapture". "The ultimate trip", Lindsey called it. We talked avidly about the rapture at youth group. The prevailing expectation was that it would come in 1981, seven years before Christ returned to judge the world and usher in a thousand year reign on earth.

Lindsey's book said we should watch for developments in Iran and, by the time I read this, Iran was already getting a lot of attention in the news. There was unrest, which led to the overthrow of the government. This confirmed in my mind that Lindsey was right about the imminence of the rapture and Armageddon. It all served to heighten my interest in what the Bible had to say about the times we were living through.

Don't believe everything you hear, my parents told me. I accepted that, but I hadn't learned to apply it to everything I should. In the next few years I got excited by books like Stan Deyo's *The Cosmic Conspiracy* and David Wilkerson's *The Vision*, which played up this expectation that something big was just around the corner, and made us hang on every word authors like that fed us. I subscribed to Keith Green's *Last Days Newsletter* and hung on every word he and his associates wrote. The result of all this was that my head was full of a lot more human teachings than Bible doctrine.

The Little Red Book

The first Bible I owned was a little red book. The Gideons came to our high school when I was in Form One (what the first year of high school was called back then), and at school assembly gave out copies of the New Testament plus Psalms and Proverbs. I was glad to get my own copy of the scriptures, but some of my class mates threw their copies away as soon as they got out of the hall. I put mine in my school bag and took it home, putting it aside somewhere.

About a year later, I decided to read it. My brother had set about reading the Bible some years earlier, and now it seemed like it was something I should do too. The little red book was in a drawer in my bedroom, and I took it out and lay in bed to read, starting at the beginning: Matthew chapter one. I honestly don't know how I got through the first seventeen verses, but I did. I reckon this showed my sincerity about reading the Good Book. I took it like medicine: I hated it, but I had to do it.   I waded through a quagmire of weird names, most of which I couldn't pronounce. I don't know how much further I got, but it can't have been far. The little red book was back in the drawer before long.

A year or so later, living in New York, I was given a bigger red book. This time it was our church which gave it, and it was the whole Bible, with some pictures and maps of the Bible lands. The church had established a practice of giving a Bible to every student in its third year high school Bible Class. I was now the proud owner of a red imitation leather Revised Standard Version, presented in a golden box (which before long had a Pink Floyd sticker stuck on the top, from their *Dark Side of the Moon* album). I kept this Bible in its box for years (taking it out occasionally), so it has lasted well. I still have it.

Then I took Confirmation Class with my church friends. At the Confirmation Ceremony, we were each presented with — you guessed it — a Bible. This time, it was a golden hardcover copy of the "Good News Bible". On this one they spelled my name correctly on the presentation page, which pleased me. This Bible didn't have photos of the Sea of Galilee etc., but it had the most fascinatingly simple but powerful illustrations, by Annie Vallotton. This became my Bible of choice. It was the most readable of the three, with its catchy drawings and section headings. It sat on top of my pile. Three Bibles! I didn't know it, but it was the start of a lifetime collection.

None of my Bibles got much use until the winter of 1978, when I was back on home turf in Australia. I started reading the gold one. The eye-catching illustrations tended to guide what I read. Among other places, they led me to the book of Ecclesiastes. "I tell you, it is all useless" was the caption under the first illustration there. As a fifteen year old, I'm sure I didn't fully grasp the message of this book, but it sure was a great book for a teenager to read. Depressing? Yes, a lot of it, but very much a "keep your feet on the ground" message. At that age, I needed to hear this wise outlook on life, especially the counsel it gives from chapter 11, verse 9 onwards. It became my favourite book in the Bible.

The Proverbs seemed a bit simplistic and pointless in the main, but there were some proverbs which stood out to me as helpful and relevant. Looking back, I can only chuckle at how much I simply didn't get. But at least I was reading God's word. I read about Jesus, and in our Bible Classes that's where most of our attention focussed, in Matthew, Mark, Luke and John.

Late in 1978, our family moved to Frankston, another bayside suburb, but 13 kilometres further south. This was a lovely place to live, but I did miss my friends and the Aspendale church gang. My parents took us to the Uniting Church, which had two congregations meeting in separate buildings on the same street. We attended the one which used to be Presbyterian. The other one used to be Methodist, and was called Wesley Uniting Church. They had their own tennis court out the back, which made me wonder.

I soon found that our new church did not subscribe to the same beliefs as the church we left. The Bible was considered a general guide, but not an authority. The miracles it reported were to be taken with a grain of salt—at least the ones you found hard to believe. So some members accepted the accounts for what they said, others accepted certain parts, but many members dismissed them as allegorical or mythological. Which ones were dismissed and which ones were believed depended on whom you spoke to.

I remember when the Uniting Church was being formed, back when I was in primary school. The idea was that three denominations (Methodist, Presbyterian and Congregationalist) were so similar in their beliefs that they should merge, and the idea of calling it "Uniting" was that the process of unification would be ongoing. Now that I was a member of this denomination (which in reality only served to create a fourth denomination, rather than uniting three existing ones), I could see that unity was an ever-receding mirage. There was a lot of talk about unity, and headlines in the church newspaper like "Call for Unity", but because different members dismissed different parts of the Bible, there was ongoing disunity. Perhaps unity under those circumstances would only be achieved if everyone totally dismissed the Bible in its entirety. But then, why be a church at all?

The minister himself said some breathtaking things from the pulpit. He seemed intent on watering down anything which might make his parishioners feel uncomfortable. One example which stands out in my mind is when he was up there in the pulpit reading the account of Jesus visiting Martha and Mary in Luke 10:38-42. "'Martha, Martha, you are anxious and troubled about many things; one thing is needful.' One dish. One dish," he explained, holding up one finger. Anyone who knows the passage will know that's not what Jesus was telling Martha, but apparently the minister wanted to avoid challenging his constituents with Christ's real point there. As I heard my father say about the good Reverend on another occasion, "Tim knows what side his bread is buttered on."

Three adults ran the youth Bible class as a discussion of social issues with little reference to the Bible, but I came along with my golden Good News Bible, and so did a few others. (The Good News Bible was the most commonly used version.) One of the leaders was an elder of the congregation, and another was his wife, a primary school principal. At this church, not only did I find the sermons unedifying, uninspiring, unbiblical and often vexing, but the Bible classes, while interesting discussions, were also not helping anyone grow in their understanding or appreciation of God's word.

I did find, mainly amongst the youth and young adults, a few who believed the Bible, including the parts where God did miracles. In fact, they believed God still empowered people to do miracles today. I certainly couldn't see why he wouldn't. But they kept their views very much to themselves, because of the prevailing belief (or rather, unbelief) in the church. Some of them even privately questioned whether the minister was a Christian. "Do you think he's saved?" one of the youth asked me. This was truly a bizarre situation to find in a church, and I found the question confronting and disturbing.

The small few who believed in modern-day miracles invited me along to some meetings of other denominations, and I found the teaching to be more Bible-based, which is what I wanted. So I began visiting these denominations whenever I had the chance. This wasn't too often, as I was still dependent upon others getting me there most of the time. My parents certainly wouldn't take me. I didn't even tell them I was going. There was the Full Blessing Church, the Assemblies of God, the Christian Revival Crusade, and some congregations of the Uniting Church where they would have what they called a "charismatic" meeting in the evening. (I later learned that this term "charismatic" was a misnomer. The more accurate term is neo-Pentecostal, but hardly anyone uses that term. I do, to avoid misapplying a biblical word which is used in Romans 12:6 to teach that every member in the body of Christ has gifts —
charismata.)

One thing a lot of these people did which I had not encountered before was to baptise by immersion, rather than sprinkling. When I was in primary school my mother had told me that some groups did that, and it seemed odd to me. But now as a teenager, meeting Bible-believing people who practised immersion, I looked at the scriptures for myself in my own time, and it was probably the first time I concluded something from own study of the scriptures.

It wasn't rocket science. I could easily see that, in the Bible, baptism was immersion in water. In John 3:23, my Good News Bible said that John was baptising "in Aenon, not far from Salim, because there was plenty of water in that place." I could see that people being baptised, as well as the one doing the baptism, "went down into the water" and "came up out of the water" (Acts 8:38-39). Even the symbolism of baptism as described in Romans 6:4-5 pointed to immersion, because Paul said, "By our baptism, then, we were buried with him and shared his death" and then "raised to life as he was" (TEV).

About this time, probably from a booklet I was loaned, I learned that the Greek word used in the scriptures for baptism actually means *immersion* or *submersion*. For reasons I could not understand, the Bible versions I was reading did not translate the word *baptizo*, but merely transliterated the word. In other words, instead of telling the reader the meaning of the word in the original text, they told the reader roughly what it sounded like. Obviously that's not going to help English readers to understand what the scriptures are telling us about baptism. It was no wonder the religious world was confused on this topic!

Getting into studying the scriptures so seriously, I found in our local religious book shop a study Bible, a big blue book, *The New English Bible, Oxford Study Edition*. It had lots of explanatory footnotes and even had the Apocrypha, which attracted me because there was more "hidden" stuff that I could delve into. It did have some helpful information in it, but it wasn't long before I found this was not my wisest purchase. There were a lot of footnotes which showed the writers did not believe a lot of what the Bible says. Still, it added to my collection of Bibles, and was easily the biggest one I had. Very impressive to turn up at a Bible study with one *that* big. Shame about the contents. I'd have been better to show up with my little red book.

Teaching Debut

It's time I told you more about that leader in the Prezzy Youth Group, the girl four years older than me. Melinda was the middle daughter of a man, Dan Milligan, who had taught me in Sunday School when I was primary school age. Mr Milligan was someone I came to respect immensely. He put a lot of time into church activities, a good example of a devout member of the church, and his whole family seemed to be active and prominent in church life.

When I, in grade three, had a question about prayer, Mr Milligan took the time after a Sunday School class to sensitively answer my question very well. It was about football. I barracked for St Kilda. They were one of the top teams, but of course they did not win every game. When St Kilda was not going well in a football match, I would pray to God to change this. I would ask God to make things go in our favour, but more often than not the match would not change to have us come out winners. Why wasn't God answering my prayers?

I'm sure you can answer that yourself, but Mr Milligan did it graciously, kindly and positively. It was the kind of man he was. Having the parents that she did, it is no surprise that Melinda also gave a lot of time and effort to church activities, particularly the youth group, and she was a caring and kind individual. She had a sincere faith which shone. She also sang and played the guitar well. Truth be told, I think I had a teenage crush on her, though I knew we were never to be an item.

She wrote me letters of encouragement when I moved to Frankston, and I was always pleased to see her when I visited Aspendale. So when I came to the conclusion that real biblical baptism was in fact immersion, I confided this to her. To my relief and encouragement, she confided to me that she had reached the same conclusion. She told me that she had raised her qualms with her minister, but he had fobbed her off, explaining it away. She wasn't satisfied with that, because she knew what the scriptures said about it. It seemed to her that people, her minister included, were just making excuses to avoid what God's word says on it.

She was not content to let theological excuses put her off. She told me she eventually found someone willing to immerse her: a minister of another denomination (the Church of Christ, who practised immersion) she met at a summer outreach program. She told me how relieved she felt to have it resolved and off her mind. It seemed that this was what I would have to do, too. It lingered in the back of my mind, this awareness that I hadn't been baptised biblically, and I decided to do it properly at some stage, when I found someone who would do it.

Meanwhile, back at the Uniting Church, the more keen ones in the Sunday Bible class were occasionally allowed to lead the discussion. In 1980 I had a chance to do this, and I taught about biblical baptism. I took them through the passages of scripture (like the ones I mentioned earlier) which showed that baptism was actually immersion. "If you see a problem with what I'm saying, shoot me down in flames."

No one did, but one of the adults, who sat listening until I had finished, said, "That might well be what they did in the first century, but it's a symbol. We mustn't lose sight of that and get hung up on what is simply a symbol."

I didn't know what to say in response. I had to agree that it was a symbol. But later I realised what I should have also said: What is it a symbol of? Romans 6:3-5 says it symbolises the death, burial and resurrection of Christ. How does sprinkling water on someone's head achieve that symbolism? Immersing someone in water — burying them, as it were, in water — powerfully symbolises Christ's death, burial and resurrection.

The Beat Goes On

Since I was in primary school, I had wanted to play the drums. I had been made to do piano lessons, but I was relieved of that misery at the end of Grade 6. I was a hopeless case when it came to trying to read music. But I never lost my interest in drums. When I was in my fourth year of high school, my sister started singing with a band. For a few months that year, I took some drumming lessons with the band's drummer at his house. I did not have my own drum set, but I had a snare drum and a practice pad, and I was able to learn the basics, including how to read drum music.

After my family had moved to Frankston, my mother came across a set of drums at a second-hand goods store, and she told me about it. She was there for something completely different, but said it was the first thing she saw when she walked in. When I walked in with her the following Saturday, I was relieved to find that they hadn't been sold. I knew little about drum sets, but this was a nice looking set, so I took it. Small, but it did the job for a beginner.

As we drove away with a set of drums squeezed into the car, my mother said, "Well it just shows that things are meant to be. It was an absolute fluke that I went into that store, and there they were." I was rapt. We had a room at the back of the house which was perfect for setting up and playing — right underneath my parents' bedroom!

As I set about getting the feel of the kit and improving my playing, an opportunity came up at the youth group I had started attending at the Uniting Church. Some of the youth were talking about forming a band. Not just a band; a church band. There were two guitarists, Rhys and Herbie, and a girl who played piano. When they found out that I played drums, they figured they had the makings of a band. It sounded good to me.

We started practising in the church hall on weekend afternoons, and some of the youth came along to sing, and before long we were playing Sunday night gigs at church. I am sure people made allowances for us, teenagers as we were, but I suppose we held our own. In fact, we must have got quite respectably good, for we were invited to play some "big gigs", like a city-wide ecumenical service hosted by the Catholic Church.

Someone came up with the idea of calling the band Agapé, from the Greek word for selfless love. I suggested Fervence, which isn't a word, but it should be. To me it suggested fervour — burning enthusiasm — without just using the word. But there wasn't any burning enthusiasm for my idea, so Agapé it was.

Occasionally I played keyboards on songs which didn't require drums or percussion, and which the pianist did not know how to play. Even though I could not read sheet music, I could play piano by ear. One of the songs I did this for was a song we brought my sister Mandy in to sing, at an outdoor multi-congregational service in a Frankston park. The song was Larry Norman's "I Am a Servant".

It was a beautiful song, and my sister sang it beautifully, so much so that the minister of our congregation wanted us to do it the following Sunday for our own congregation. Mandy was busy elsewhere, so it didn't happen, but something bothered me about the idea anyway. In hindsight, I think it was the entertainment factor driving this request. *The song was a hit at the outdoor concert, so let's do an encore for the home crowd, kids. It'll blow them away!* (Shades of Pink Floyd's "Have a Cigar".)

When you're in the midst of all this, you really don't take time to stop and consider why you're doing it, and what (if anything) it has to do with the message Jesus brought to earth. If you pick up the New Testament and read it, is there anything remotely like what we were doing in there? We spent hours practising on our own and rehearsing together, and then we went on with the show, but where was Jesus in all this? Where was the glory going? We seemed to have confused self-sacrifice with self-aggrandisement, but in all sincerity and naïvety I saw it as my service for God — because I never stopped to look at what God actually says he wants us to do to serve him. It's a trap I can still fall into, but I'm more conscious of it now, having learned the grave implications of Matthew 7:21-23.

> Not everyone who says to me, "Lord, Lord," will enter the kingdom of heaven, but he who does the will of my Father who is in heaven. Many will say to me in that day, "Lord, Lord, did we not prophesy in your name, and in your name we cast out demons, and in your name we did many mighty works?" And then I will confess to them, "I never knew you! Depart from me, you who work iniquity!"

There really is a big difference between doing what you consider to be a service for the Lord, and doing what he says.

During this period, I was into a couple of religious musicians in a big way. Larry Norman was the main one, because he was usually more hard-edged. Keith Green was the other, and I had been to one of his concerts in Melbourne. One of his songs was called "To Obey is Better Than Sacrifice," from the album *No Compromise*. That song played a key part in preparing me to submit to what God tells us all to do—to obey him. I played it a lot on the piano, singing it to myself.

The lyrics on the album sleeve had a scripture reference above them. It was 1 Samuel 15:22-23, the passage which had inspired the song. In my golden Good News Bible I found it and learned the sober lesson the chapter presented about what it meant to obey the Lord. King Saul had partially done what God had commanded him, but God makes it clear that partial obedience is not obedience. That's just doing what suits you. "I did obey the Lord," Saul insisted. "But..."

> Samuel said, "Which does the Lord prefer: obedience or offerings and sacrifices? It is better to obey than to sacrifice the best sheep to him. Rebellion against him is as bad as witchcraft, and arrogance is as sinful as idolatry. Because you have rejected the Lord's command, he has rejected you as king."[6]

---

[6] 1 Samuel 15:22-23 (TEV)

This was not an account I knew anything about before I heard Keith Green's song. The song was not about what had happened in King Saul's day, but about what was happening in our day, in churches everywhere.

To obey is better than sacrifice
I don't need your money, I want your life
And I hear you say that I'm coming back soon
But you act like I'll never return

Well you speak of grace and my love so sweet
How you thrive on milk but reject my meat
And I can't help weeping at how it will be
If you keep on ignoring my words

To my mind, this was a song we needed to play in church. Or rather, our audience needed us to play this in church. My mother did not agree, when I sat her down in our loungeroom to listen to the song and read the lyrics on the album sleeve as the song played. She had asked me what other songs (besides "I Am a Servant") I knew which might be suitable either for Mandy to sing or Agapé to perform. This song was first on my list, but Mum said "Oh, I don't agree with that. That's too extreme," when she saw words like these:

To obey is better than sacrifice
I want more than Sundays and Wednesday nights
'Cause if you can't come to me every day
Then don't bother coming at all

To obey is better than sacrifice
I want hearts of fire, not your prayers of ice
And I'm coming quickly to give back to you
According to what you have done
According to what you have done
According to what you have done[7]

----

[7] To Obey is Better Than Sacrifice, Keith Green, ©1978 Birdwing Music (Admin. by Universal Music Publishing MGB Australia Pty Limited)

I knew it wouldn't float with my fellow band-members, either — at least most of them. Plus there was the problem that it required keyboards and drums, and our pianist did not know how to play the song, unless we found the sheet music somewhere. It just wasn't going to get off the ground.

Another song by Keith Green which pointed me in the right direction was "Unless the Lord Builds the House". It didn't have the same impact on me as "To Obey", but it certainly put to the front of my mind the importance of doing what God wants me to do, not just what I think he would like. This song's key thought was drawn from Psalm 127.

> *Unless the Lord builds the house*
> *They labour in vain who try at all*
> *In building anything not according to his call*
> *Unless the Lord wants it done*
> *You better not work another day*
> *Building anything that will stand in His way*

A bit further on it said:

> *But are you so sure you're not just doing what you want to*
> *Building your house on the sand?*[8]

There it was again: Matthew 7, where Jesus warns his listeners about calling him "Lord" but not doing what he says. Those who do that, Christ likens to the fool who built his house on the sand, in contrast to those who hear him and obey him.

> So then, anyone who hears these words of mine and obeys them is like a wise man who built his house on rock. The rain poured down, the rivers flooded over, and the wind blew hard against that house. But it did not fall, because it was built on rock.

---

[8] *Unless the Lord Builds the House*, Keith & Melody Green, ©1980 Birdwing Music ASCAP

But anyone who hears these words of mine and does not obey them is like a foolish man who built his house on sand. The rain poured down, the rivers flooded over, the wind blew hard against that house, and it fell. And what a terrible fall that was![9]

I knew what these passages said, and I loved the songs which challenged me to put God's word into practice. The test would be whether I was willing to give up anything to obey the Lord, even playing in a church band.

Seeking a Sign

Spending time around friends who believed God was still distributing gifts of the Holy Spirit to people, and reading about those gifts in the scriptures, had its natural effect on me: I set my heart on spiritual gifts, just as 1 Corinthians 14:1 urged. Being able to heal people was a gift I especially liked the sound of, but there was also the gift of "faith" and "the working of miracles", among a whole buffet of goodies listed in 1 Corinthians 12:4-11. These were the three topping my wish list.

Somehow I got the idea that, with the gift of faith supercharging my faith, I would be able to levitate. I mean, if a tiny mustard seed of faith could empower you to move a mountain[10], then a body floating a few centimetres off the floor was a pushover. Nobody I knew suggested that to me; it was entirely my invention, perhaps inspired by hearing about Indian gurus who claimed to levitate. It was one of my main requests of God, that he lift me off the floor. The first time would be the hardest because, never having done it before, I would have an element of doubt in my mind. But once I'd floated over that hurdle, the next times would be no trouble at all.

Naturally, I had to be alone for this. My parents or siblings would freak out. I didn't know what it would be like, either, so it was best kept to myself until I got the hang of it. I was staying at my grandmother's house in Rosebud one time, and when she was out I decided it was the perfect opportunity to make the breakthrough. I prayed earnestly, with the heart pumping, standing in the middle of her loungeroom. The emotion welled, the arms twitched and jerked…but my feet stayed firmly on the carpet. Probably a good thing, really, as her house didn't have a high ceiling.

Despite believing so sincerely and fervently, I never did receive what I was asking for. I put it down to lack of faith. In later years I learned that it wasn't so much a lack of faith as it was putting faith in the wrong thing. The faith Jesus was talking about was faith in God and what he says. My burning faith was in my own idea that

---

[10] Matthew 17:20-21; 21:21-22

God would do something which he had never promised me. I was misunderstanding and misapplying things I read in scripture, and later I learned that biblical faith "comes by hearing, and hearing by the word of God"[11] — not by dreaming up your own ideas, or following some fallible human's ideas.

Of the people I knew who believed that God still gave gifts of the Spirit, they all believed that God had given them the gift of speaking in tongues. This seemed odd to me, because I could see in the scriptures that God said "he gives a different gift to each person"[12]. So why was he giving tongues to everyone? Why couldn't I have healing, or miracles, or faith? Some of the churches I visited taught that speaking in tongues, at least once, was a sign that you were filled with the Holy Spirit. So with all of this around me, it was inevitable that I would desire this gift that the others had. I figured I might as well seek a lesser gift, and the one at the bottom of the list was the gift of speaking in tongues. I didn't feel a part of the club without it.

Over and over I read all the passages I could find which related to speaking in tongues.[13] This gave me a very clear picture of what it was, and what I should expect when God gave me the gift. I could see it was the ability to speak languages which the speaker had never learned, purely by the power of the Spirit. I could see that it came unexpectedly upon people at first, but that people with the gift had control of when they would use it. One thing I did notice was that my big blue Bible, the New English Bible, put a totally different term in 1 Corinthians 12–14. It said "ecstatic utterance" instead of speaking in tongues. The other versions just translated it as it is, "speak in tongues", but the NEB brazenly substituted words which had nothing to do with the words of the original text. It was one of the reasons I came to dislike that translation: it took huge liberties with the text. But it also made me aware that I needed to compare translations, as some showed a bias which could mislead a truth-seeker.

---

[11] Romans 10:17

[12] 1 Corinthians 12:11 (TEV)

[13] Mark 16:17; Acts 1:8; 2:1-21; 10:44-47; 19:1-7; 1 Cor 12 – 14

Knowing what I knew from the scriptures about the gift of tongues, I prayed just as fervently for that gift as I had prayed to be lifted off the ground. I knew what to expect, but it didn't come. I didn't tell anyone about this, though. It was better to let them assume I could speak in tongues than admit God hadn't given me the gift. It was an unspoken attitude in those circles that if you couldn't at least speak in tongues, you were a second-rate Christian. There were some (not in my circle) who even believed you were not saved without it. I kept praying, and I kept quiet.

Around this time, in Year Eleven at school, I took up football umpiring with the Southern Umpires Association. I went to training with my brother two nights a week, and officiated as a boundary umpire on Saturdays in one of three local footy leagues. When you started learning to umpire, you started on the boundaries. You also started with reserve grade matches. Only when you were assessed to be good enough did you get assigned to senior matches. Being a young first-year recruit, that was a little way off yet.

In those days, because umpires had to run more than anyone else on the footy field, they had to be the fittest on the field. We did not have to train in all the skills of Australian Football; we simply had to be excellent runners (forwards and backwards) who knew how to bounce a football and throw it in from the boundary. This meant our training was quite straightforward (and backwards), and I was as fit then as I have ever been. But in mid-season I developed a problem with my shins and ankles. The pain I was experiencing in my legs meant I had to put myself on the injured list. I can't recall how many weeks I missed umpiring in matches, but I *can* recall how I got back to match fitness.

During the school holidays I stayed overnight at my school friend Peter's house and took him to a Wednesday night meeting of the local "CRC" — Christian Revival Crusade. It wasn't far from his house. At this meeting, a woman who was, so I had been told, renowned as a healer stood up to speak to us. I did not think anything unusual about this; I was used to women addressing congregations, and I had never noticed passages of scripture like 1 Timothy 2:11-14 which forbid this. This lady's name was Nina Hooper, and she spoke pretty well. She wasn't hyper, she didn't rant; she just spoke about spiritual things, which was something we at the Uniting Church were starved of. (My friend was a Catholic and, from what I had seen, I imagine he experienced the same.) After Nina had finished speaking, people who needed healing were invited to come forward for her to pray for them. I took my legs to the front.

As I stood waiting for Nina to get to me, I watched her go and speak quietly to each person, then put her hands on them. When she did this, the person would fall backwards and be caught by a man standing behind them, who lowered them gently to the floor. I had seen this plenty of times, and I did not fancy the idea of falling backwards. When she came to me, she gently asked, "What would you like me to pray for?"

"My ankles and my shins," I said, my voice betraying how nervous I was.

"Sure," she said. "Just close your eyes and fix your thoughts on Jesus."

I closed my eyes and felt her touch the outside of my calves. As she did, what felt like a mild electric current passed across my lower legs. Then I fell lightly back into the arms of the man waiting behind me, and ended up on the floor. I was euphoric, and I lay there with my eyes closed praying to God. I was sure now was the time God was going to zap me with the gift of tongues. After laying there some time, trying to work up the excitement to usher in the great moment, I got up without any power coming upon me.

Afterwards I spoke to a man who looked a little like Buddy Holly, and had been walking around saying something like, "Leeger lager leeger lager leeger lager." We were in the room behind the front of the meeting hall, and Nina was continuing to pray for people, and do things with them you would expect a physiotherapist to do with her patients. I got talking to this man, and he asked, "Have you been baptised in the Holy Spirit?"

I confided in this man whom I had never met before, telling him what I had not told any of my friends. "I've been asking God to give me the gift of tongues, but I haven't received it yet. I really don't know why."

He looked thoughtful and said, "That *is* strange. I don't know why you wouldn't receive it, because if the desire is there, and you ask in faith, he says you will receive it." This man had the same misguided view of prayer (as well as gifts of the Spirit) that I had, so we were both perplexed about my situation.

I said, "Well, I've been asking."

He said, "You looked like you were going to receive it when you were praying on the floor before. Would you like me to pray for you about it?"

"Sure," I said, and he stood in front of me and put his hands on my shoulders.

He didn't say anything in his prayer except what sounded like, "Leeger lager leeger lager leeger lager." Meanwhile, I got excited again, expecting to receive what I had read about in the New Testament. After a while of nothing happening, the man said, "Just say what I'm saying".

"Leeger lager leeger lager leeger lager," I said.

"Now just let it flow from yourself."

I let it flow. In a matter of moments I was saying things which were definitely not English. This was it! I was speaking in tongues! I was so excited I was up in a flash, and hugged Peter who was nearby. (He later said that it was a very strong hug, and that I was hugging everybody.) After all that time praying, I was elated that I had finally received the gift. In all my rapture I totally overlooked that what had just happened was not what I had read about in the New Testament. I was expecting what the scriptures described, but got something quite different. People in the first century were not taught to speak in other tongues. They were "filled with the Holy Spirit and began to speak in other languages, as the Spirit enabled them to speak."[14] But the emotion of the moment totally obscured that from my thoughts.

The next morning I had a dentist appointment for a check up. Peter tagged along, and came upstairs to sit in the waiting room. It didn't take long, and as we were about to go back downstairs to the street, I began to step down carefully, as I had done on stairs for a few weeks, because of my injury. Then I thought: *Hang on. I've been healed. I don't need to do this anymore.* Off I bounded down the stairs, all the way to the street footpath. Not a touch of pain! I was healed! I turned to Peter and told him what had just happened. It was amazing and thrilling, and I gave God the glory — as I should have.

As soon as I could, I resumed training, and umpiring football matches. My legs and ankles gave me no trouble, and I was able to finish out the season without any problem. I did begin to notice some pain in my legs after a couple of weeks. I thought to myself that this was because I had kept on doing what had injured my legs, so the same problem was developing again after God had healed it — just like if you get a car fully repaired, then go and continue driving it into brick walls.

When I told Rhys, the guitarist in our band who was neo-Pentecostal, about this, he said, "Are you saying that God does a lousy repair job?"

I said, "No, I'm saying he did a perfect job, but I'm damaging it again."

"Rubbish! God doesn't do a second-rate job. Satan wants us to think he does, but when God heals, he heals completely." Rhys was very adamant in his beliefs, whatever the topic. "Do you believe that?"

"Sure he does."

"Well don't let Satan tell you any different. He'll do whatever he can to fool you into doubting God."

---

[14] Acts 2:4 (TEV)

With Rhys' reassurance in mind, when I felt twinges of pain after that, my response was: *Get behind me, Satan! I know you're trying to fool me into thinking that God hasn't healed me. But I know he has.* That would relieve things for a while, but the pain returned and grew. Eventually, psyching myself that I wasn't really feeling pain didn't work any longer. I didn't understand why at the time. Later on, when I grew in my faith and understanding of the scriptures, I realised the truth of what I had experienced: my legs were not miraculously healed. I was psychosomatically healed — well, at least relieved. It does go to show what a marvellous mind God has given us. It's a more powerful tool than we realise.

As for Nina the healer, I cannot say whether she used any trickery to make me feel that 'electric' feeling. I do not know whether she was knowingly deceitful or sincerely misguided, and whether that feeling was just the result of my keen anticipation. The few times I heard her speak, she struck me as a sincere person with a zeal for God, and I prefer to think of her that way. Whatever the case, for a good while I remained convinced that God had healed me and that he had empowered me to speak in another language. I had no idea that God had a much bigger work to do in me yet — something genuine and lasting.

Glossolalia

Because I had let my holy-roller friends assume that I could speak in tongues, I did not tell them about Wednesday night's turn of events. Well, I did tell them about the healing, but not what happened after that. Alone in my bedroom, I would quietly try out this new gift I (thought I) had. It gave me a thrill to do it. God had finally given me a spiritual gift! Any doubt that I had been filled with the Holy Spirit was now put to rest; he was speaking through me. This confirmed to me that God was powerfully at work in my life, and it lifted me.

Eventually, I confided in a select few that I could speak in tongues. Three of us in the youth group used to get together to pray in a back room of the church hall. I told them, because we had talked about tongues-speaking, and they had each told me they could do it. So, once we all knew that we all shared the same gift, we not only prayed together in English, we "prayed in tongues" together also. This was the only time I would do this in front of someone else.

In actual fact, I *had* done it in front of someone else, years before, but that did not occur to me in all my excitement of believing I could speak in tongues. I used to talk gibberish in early high school. My English school friend Jeremy and I used to amuse ourselves by walking along the street and pretending to speak a foreign language as someone approached from the other direction. Of course, you had to sound convincing, and that took some practice. The more you practise, the more convincing you can sound. (At least we thought so.) It's not hard to do, but in my experience some are better at it than others. In my opinion, the key is to put expression into your babble, and avoid excessive repetition of sounds.

A few years later, once I was taught to "speak in tongues" at the CRC, I did exactly the same thing as I used to do with my friend Jeremy. And the more I practised, the more convincing I sounded. That's not the way I thought of it at the time. I genuinely believed I was speaking another language. Only when I grew in faith later, away from the neo-Pentecostal crowd, did I see the connection of my "tongues" experience with my earlier faking game.

My study of scriptures like Acts 2:1-12 and 1 Corinthians 12–14 showed me that people who were empowered by the Holy Spirit to speak in different tongues were speaking real languages. In fact, some translations render the word "tongues" as "languages". In 1 Corinthians 14:18 Paul said, "I thank my God I speak with tongues more than you all." So Paul, one man, spoke with tongues; not a tongue, but tongues – plural. This is why, when you count the places people came from in Acts 2:9-11, those places[15] outnumber the men who were speaking in those local dialects. There were only twelve apostles there, all Galileans,[16] but more than twelve languages were spoken, because the gift they were given was to "speak in different languages, as the Spirit gave them utterance." One gifted individual could speak whatever languages the Spirit spoke through them.

This is not the idea I picked up from fellow neo-Pentecostals. They talked about being given "a tongue". Rather than believing that we could speak in tongues, we believed that we could speak in a tongue – even though we called it "tongues". One of my friends said, "I've been given a very gruff-sounding tongue. It sounds like a middle eastern language, maybe Afghan; I don't know." I didn't know what my "tongue" sounded like, but if I had kept my head on straight I would have realised that I should have been speaking "various kinds of tongues"[17] which would sound quite different to each other. But, as I have said, I had lost sight of the biblical teaching in all the euphoria of being convinced that I could speak in tongues, that God's power was at work in me.

In hindsight I can see that God *was* working powerfully and purposefully in my life, but not in the way I had thought.

---

[15] I do think it likely that Luke only gives us a sampling of the places people had come from. There were probably people from other places as well, but this was enough to make his point.

[16] Acts 2:7. Thus we can confirm that this wasn't a gathering of all 120 disciples, for we know there were non-Galilean disciples then.

[17] 1 Corinthians 12:10 (ESV)

The Making of a Skeptic

"People have been putting up with mosquitoes for tens of *thous*ands of years. You can put up with them for one week."

My father seemed quite proud of his statement. He resumed shaving with a quiet chuckle. It was one summer in my childhood, and I had been stressing over the fact that we had run out of insecticide—fly spray, we called it—and we would not be buying any until shopping day the following week. This was dreadful news. Mosquitoes traumatised my nights. I would hide my head under the sheet and hear them massing around me, baying for blood.

In my despondent acceptance of the fact that I would have to face the mozzies without chemical weapons, I did not bat an eyelid at the premise forming the background of my father's statement. I had grown up being taught that the world was millions of years old. It was the prevailing worldview of our day, and we all accepted it without question. I had not encountered at church any suggestion that this could be even slightly wrong.

Fast forward to 1979, my first year at Frankston High School. I heard about a "Christian Fellowship Group" which would meet at lunchtime once a week, and I decided to go along to check it out. A woman from the Baptist Church was there, and she handed out a little comic book called "Have You Been Brainwashed?" and talked about it. I had no idea what she was on about. Perhaps because most there understood what she was talking about, she did not start at square one, and that is where I was. She was speaking as if there was a conflict between the Bible and what was commonly believed about the origin of life on earth. I had certainly never heard of such a conflict. No one at either the Presbyterian or Uniting Churches had even mentioned it, as far as I could recall.

I took the little comic booklet home but, not being a fan of comics, I did not give it much of a look. This did, however, open me up to an awareness that there was some dissent on this topic. It was not until the following year that I gave it serious consideration. I was in the senior school library when I came across a book on the shelf written by Dr Duane T Gish. It was called "Evolution? The Fossils Say No!"[18] Who would have put a book like that in a high school library? There must have been someone on staff who did not accept the popular notion that life came from non-life by itself and evolved into the array of species we have today. I know that one of the teachers at the school was a devout Baptist. Maybe it was him, but I really don't know.

I flicked through this book, knowing it was taking the line that I had heard the year before from that woman. I decided to borrow it so that I could get a better look at it. At home I also pulled out the "Brainwashed" comic and gave that a closer look. It was a shocking eye-opener that there was a whole mass of facts which we were not being told at school, or on the television. It came at a time when I had already found points of disagreement with the line taught at my family's church, and this turned out to be another point on which I came to differ with them.

In Year 11 English we were learning about "clear thinking": analysing and critiquing arguments. I loved this, as it helped me assess the arguments heatedly put at our family's dinner table. These arguments were usually sparked by something in the news, especially politics. Sitting at our table, I saw all the fallacious methods of argument we were learning about at school. I could pick them, but I seldom weighed in. Most family arguments were a spectator sport for me. The favourite method of putting a point strongly in our family was to raise one's voice. It taught me to appreciate Cicero's observation that "Orators are most vehement when they have the weakest cause, as men get on horseback when they cannot walk."

Typical of most teenagers, I questioned a lot of the things my parents held to be true. For example, I had heard them confidently affirm for as long as I could remember, that when you have sunburn, the best thing for it is to have a hot shower. "It takes the

---

[18] Gish, Duane T., *Evolution? The Fossils Say No!* (Creation-Life Publishers, San Diego, 1973) It was probably the second edition of the book I saw, back then.

heat out of it." I tried it and tried it as a child, but it never worked. It just hurt. "You don't have the water hot enough," my parents would tell me. So I would try it again with even hotter water, to no avail.

When Mr Kaplan, my Year 9 science teacher, told us that one way of viewing the temperature of any object (or "mass") was its ability to absorb heat, it made good sense to me. But as I applied that to things like subjecting your already glowing hot skin to even hotter water, it dawned on me that the claim, "It takes the heat out", was a load of rubbish. What my burned back needed, if anything, was *cold* water, not hot. To use one of my father's favourite expressions, "Blind Freddy could see that!" I don't know how traditions like this start, but I imagine this one could have begun with a bunch of blokes in a pub, pulling their sunburnt mate's leg for a lark. If we don't question such traditions — intelligently, not blindly rejecting them — we suffer for it. We would still be cutting people open to bleed away their illness.

So it's things like this that make you realise your parents are not as wise as you once thought. Teenagers are good at realising this. I am sure I overestimated my parents' stupidity, but at least I was questioning what I had always held to be true. That is what true skepticism is: it questions what purports to be truth.[19] Now, in Year 11, I was questioning a very basic tenet of my parents' worldview, the question of human existence: where did we come from?

That year, two of my subjects were Biology and Earth Science, and by the time we got to the second half of the year, when the General Theory of Evolution was really strongly pushed, I was no longer a believer. I made my skepticism known in my written assignments. The biology teacher, Mr Wilcox, seemed to be used to this sort of occasional resistance, and he knew how to handle a young upstart like me, so I never made any headway. I had only just woken up to the failings of evolutionary theory, and was still getting used to thinking along different lines to how I had been raised.

---

[19] The Macquarie Dictionary (Macquarie Library, McMahons Point, 1981)

One lunchtime, I quietly went into the biology classroom and wrote on the blackboard (which was actually green):

"I was only joking!" — Charles Darwin, 1882

I pulled the board so that it was obscured, and would only appear when the teacher was in full flight with a class. The next day, I saw Mr Wilcox and said, "They tell me he was only joking."

"Who's that?" he asked, not catching on.

"Darwin," I added.

"Did you? — oh..." His expression turned from surprise to a smile which said *You little smart-alec.*

Over the next couple of years I explored a range of alternatives to the beliefs under which I had been raised. The Clear Thinking classes had freed me to critically question everything political, religious, and ideological. I found in our local city library some fascinating reading. *Existentialism is a Humanism*, by Jean-Paul Satre, was one I recall taking my interest. Absorbing reading, but it failed to deal with a basic and fatal flaw in its logic, as far as I could see: claiming that "truth is subjective", one has to have an objective basis for that claim. In other words, how can you declare the truth that there is no such thing as absolute truth?

Another writer I found at the Library was Anthony Flew, a celebrated champion of Atheism. He wrote quite derisively of religious explanations for our existence, but it seemed he was never able to answer the question of the first cause, and the origin of life itself. His main thrust was to depict those who attributed these things to God as being superstitious or given to childish fantasies. That didn't explain the elephant in the room: what caused the universe to be here, how did it form into such complex order and how did life appear in the first place? Decades later, Mr Flew did finally come to terms with those questions when he concluded "There is a God."[20]

Looking back, it is not surprising that it was during this period I was converted. Being open to consider things which differ to one's own beliefs is crucial in a search for truth. I did not end up rejecting Christ or God, but the version of Christianity in which I had been raised. Christ's credentials stood up to the closest scrutiny. It was Churchianity that failed to. But I'm getting ahead of myself.

---

[20] There Is a God: How the World's Most Notorious Atheist Changed His Mind (Harper Collins, New York, 2007)

Jackie and Jacko

At Frankston High School I got to know more Baptists than at any other stage of my life. I did not know much about Baptist beliefs, except that they actually baptised people, rather than just christening them. But I did see, in the Baptists I got to know at school, a faith much more like mine than I saw in most at the Uniting Church. In their circle, I began to be influenced in their direction. Plus of course, their literature dominated the shelves of religious bookshops.

Among the tracts which I collected was one called "Have you Heard of the Four Spiritual Laws?" It was written by an evangelical and used by evangelicals to convert people. I liked the way it summed the message we wanted to get across to the lost, and it certainly helped people like me who didn't know our way around the Bible. It did the work for us; we would just have to read through the tract with the one we were trying to convert.

I went with some people in our church to a training seminar on how to use this little tract to "witness" to people. The most daunting thing about that whole seminar was that we actually went out and knocked on doors to speak to people, using the tract. To break the ice, we started with a "We're doing a survey" spiel. It was a bit like push-polling: we asked questions which led to the cruncher, "Have you heard of the four spiritual laws?" We didn't make any converts.

The tract taught that "you can receive Christ right now by faith through prayer", and it contained a suggested prayer for the sinner to pray. I had never heard this taught before reading that tract. My background in the Presbyterian Church, as I said earlier, gave me the idea that you became a Christian as faith blossomed. At some stage you crossed the line into being a child of God. This tract actually outlined a specific point. Although I had never heard this taught before, it did not strike me as anything bad. I had never helped anyone become a Christian before, so what would I know?

Then a girl in our year named Trudy, a Baptist, got talking with her friend Jackie about Christianity. Jackie decided that she wanted to become a Christian, and Trudy rounded up the church-goers to tell us this happy news. We sat in a circle in the school yard and Trudy explained to Jackie that you become a Christian by praying to Jesus. Then she asked *me* to lead the prayer for Jackie to repeat! This came out of the blue, and perhaps it was because I was the only male sitting there. (I can't recall.) I was put on the spot, but I did roughly know what the prayer in that tract said, so I led her through a repeat-after-me prayer. We all rejoiced with her that she was now saved, and Trudy continued Jackie's induction into Christianity. I only wish I knew then what I came to know in the next couple of years. It would have been so much better for Jackie. By the time I learned how unbiblical this all was, Jackie had left school.

The year following Jackie's conversion, Jacko came to our school. IIe only stayed one year, but I became good friends with him. We shared the same zany sense of humour (as one of my teachers described it), and he too showed interest in becoming a Christian. This time another Baptist, Rick, took the lead in telling Jacko about Christianity. Rick was a very forthright individual; you were left in no doubt what he believed. Perhaps 'headstrong' is a more apt word for him. By the time Jacko (as we called him) had finished his year at our school, he had himself a Bible and was convinced that Jesus was the Son of God, but he had not become a member of any church. We kept in touch, and still hung out together after Year 11 had finished. There were big things to come in our lives before long.

The Search for a Church

One day when I was sixteen years old I was standing on my own in our family room, near the heater, going over the situation I was in. Because of my parents, I was attending a church which I found frustratingly disinterested in what the scriptures taught—even resistant to it. I felt isolated from my family because of my beliefs. Standing there, I told myself, "When I'm eighteen, *I'll* decide what church I go to. It'll be *my* choice." By this stage I had already been visiting denominations which I found to be far more appealing than the Uniting Church. Now I resolved to check out as many denominations as I could, so that when I turned eighteen I could start attending a more scriptural church.

I checked out all the denominations I could find, except the Mormons, JWs and Catholics. I already knew enough about them. When we played that "big gig" at the big catholic Church, I saw all the statues and how members had to bow their heads to the main one at the front of the chapel. Out of respect for their beliefs, I genuflected respectfully as well. It was quaint and amusing, but not appealing in the least to me. Those statues and pictures looked positively creepy. The priest was too. Very unfriendly.

The Mormons came to our door every so often, so I had an idea of what they were about. They were always trying to interest people in their own sacred book, the Book of Mormon, and an American who claimed to be a prophet of God. I think it was Rick who loaned me a book called, "Counterfeits at Your Door" which explained the beliefs of JWs and Mormons, and how they differed from Baptist thinking. (While it educated me in those beliefs, it also influenced me further towards Baptist doctrine as well, though I didn't notice at the time.)

The Anglicans did not appeal to me much either. I knew some nice people who went to one of their congregations, and I attended a few home groups with them. But there was a certain stuffy establishment feel to the Anglican Churches I visited. They were tied up in their own traditions, rather than wanting to learn from the Bible. Plus the whole concept of "The Church of England" seemed about as bizarre to me as the Mormons' American prophet.

Other denominations in town which I visited were:

- Christian & Missionary Alliance — they seemed pretty standard evangelicals, but they lacked the joy I saw in other groups.
- Church of Christ — basically the same as the Uniting Church, except they were a little more contemporary, and they immersed rather than sprinkled (because they paid a bit more attention to the Bible). I met some nice people there, but the church was more sedate than Pentecostal, for my liking.[21]
- 'Gospel Chapel' Brethren — a weird experience, where we all sat in silence, with at least one reading a book in his pew, until someone in the congregation stood up and shared a thought they had had, then resumed his seat, and we waited in silence until someone else stood up with something to say.
- Full Blessing Church — the full blessing, they believed, was being filled with the Spirit. Their meetings were marked by too much emotionalism and not enough intelligent discourse for my liking.
- Christian Revival Crusade — I attended here more than other denominations, and met a lot of really lovely people. Their youth group was a fair size, and they were enthusiastic. I once saw a bunch of their youth parading through the main shopping district of Frankston, *hare Krishna* style, but joyfully singing to a ghetto blaster which was blasting out a gospel song. I loved that!
- Baptists — even though they had a 'reputation', they were pretty appealing to me. They seemed switched on and enthusiastic.

I suppose they all had their good points and bad points, and certainly there were nice people in all of them. The Baptists and CRC were the most likely contenders. I was looking for somewhere that recognised and practised the gifts of the Holy Spirit, and the Baptists fell rather short there. But while the CRC were fine on this front, I could see there was too much emotionalism at play in their

---

[21] By "Church of Christ" I mean the denomination using that term as its name. I am aware that many congregations of New Testament Christians call themselves this, too, but they are not affiliated with this denomination.

meetings. This was something that bothered me about all the neo-Pentecostal denominations that I had visited: they all depended upon whipping up the emotions, and they tended to ignore the instructions of 1 Corinthians 14 about how to exercise the gifts in their assemblies. But both Baptists and CRC paid more attention to the Bible than others I had checked out, and that was a major plus from my point of view. I was, after all, trying to find a more scriptural church.

That's the way I put it when I visited a denomination, if somebody asked me. I was "looking for a more scriptural church". My girlfriend usually came with me when I visited, and she affirmed the same thing. But really, she was heading in a different direction, and she was pulling me that way too. She did have a faith, but her heart was being hardened and lured by the deceitfulness of sin.[22] The more I resisted, pulling in the other direction, the more antagonistic she became. As much as I wish that relationship had ended sooner, one thing about it makes me glad.

It happened in her kitchen. I never went near the local newspaper. I don't think my parents did, either, until election time. But my girlfriend's mother did, and she would read the church notices. She knew that I was visiting different churches, looking for a more scriptural one, so as she sat at her table reading the paper, she said, "This sounds interesting. There's a group trying to restore the teaching and practices of the church as read in the New Testament. It says, 'Anyone interested in simple New Testament Christianity is most welcome'."

It sounded exactly like what I was looking for. I had a look at the notice, and it invited people "to an informal Bible Study at 39 Heatherhill Rd., Frankston, at 8 p.m. Tuesday nights. For further details, phone 781 4660." I was on the phone in a flash, and a man with an English accent answered. I didn't catch his name but he sounded friendly, and by the time I hung up I was determined to get there on a Tuesday night. That address was in easy walking distance from my house; even better if I rode my bike.

---

[22] Hebrews 3:13

Being late September, the local football season had recently finished so I no longer had umpire training on Tuesday nights, which would make it easier to visit. I got there on a night early in October, my girlfriend in tow. We walked into the loungeroom of an old house, and met two couples, the Pollocks and the Jackmans. Jeff and Patricia Pollock, with their three young girls, had just moved to Frankston and bought this house, and the Jackmans had not long been in Frankston either. That's all the adults there were, and the children soon went to bed, leaving just six of us. It was not easy for a 17 year old introvert to walk in on this situation, so I was glad I had someone with me. But I soon found they were friendly and easy-going people, so it was a pleasant evening. We had a common love for God and his word, which made for an instant rapport. However, there was no hint that they believed they had gifts of the Spirit, as I had expected and hoped, so I left wondering what they believed on that.

What impressed me most about the evening was the actual Bible study. We were in John chapter one, and I think I learned more in one night than I was used to learning in 30. The teacher, Jeff, obviously knew his Bible, and had studied the passage well to present a truly informative and edifying class. The sort of "Bible study" I was used to was one where the leader typically would ask some questions and we would all pool our ignorance. But this night I came away like people came away from Jesus: "They all ate and were filled." I was keen to go back, just as the crowds came back to Jesus for more food, but with the school year winding up, my parents would not allow me to go out every Tuesday night until exams were finished. I knew this without asking.

I did go back, and grew to love visiting that old house. It had been a rundown shack, but Jeff was fixing it up with the help of his father. Of course, it was the people, not the house that attracted me. This humble abode was filled with love. There was a slightly chaotic feel, with the three children and their dog Scamp frolicking about the place, but I felt relaxed and welcomed there. (The house is gone now, not surprisingly.)

Soon after that night I first visited the Pollocks' house, the next big turn in my life came. One might think it was Satan throwing a spanner in the works, but I see in hindsight that God was ensuring that Satan would not thwart my search.

A Child Left to Himself

My parents left home when I was seventeen. Late in 1980, soon after I met those two Christian couples, our family learned that my father was to be transferred by his employer, the ANZ Bank, to manage a city branch in Sydney. Our house had to go on the market, and our comfortable existence in Frankston was to come to an end after only two years.

My brother and sister had jobs in the Melbourne CBD, so they decided to rent a flat closer to the city. Ordinarily I would have moved with my parents, as we did to New York some years earlier. But I was lined up to do my final year of high school, to obtain the coveted Higher School Certificate. That left me with a dilemma. It was best to stay on at the same school and complete my HSC as, all things considered, that gave me the best chance of success. Undertaking HSC at another school, especially one in a different state, would be a handicap. (I also didn't want to leave my girlfriend, but I left that unsaid.)

The dilemma was that I had nowhere to stay. If I could not find anywhere, then I would have no choice but to move to Sydney. A notice was put in the newsletter of our church, and also the neighbouring Wesley Uniting Church, asking if anyone was able to have a student board with them while he did HSC. It was in the newsletters for a few weeks, with no response. Then my mother received a phone call, and I was in the house to hear it. We had a bite! I heard Mum talking about me, saying, "He's quite a conservative boy." Interesting selling point: she was probably banking on a common aversion to punks with pins through their ears and eyebrows.

Mum was talking to Mrs Wilks, a widow who lived in Frankston, who had a friend at the Wesley Uniting Church. That's how she had heard about this boy needing board. A meeting was arranged at her house, where I would go by myself and we would introduce ourselves. She had an ideal house for boarding. Three bedrooms, with her room on the other side of the house from the other two, with its own *en suite*. That meant privacy for both of us, and a bathroom of my own. The window of the bedroom which I would use also had a glass door which opened onto the back courtyard. To top it off, Mrs Wilks also had a Golden Labrador named Ella. What more could I want?

Mrs Wilks and I were both shy, so it was a tad awkward, but I passed the interview. She agreed to have me. With that settled, I could get on with finishing out the year at school, packing up my belongings, and preparing for HSC in Melbourne.

With all that occupying my life, I did not give a lot of time to visiting those four Christians, or any church. My last visit before I went with my parents to spend the summer in Sydney was during December of 1980. School had finished, and I took the opportunity to see what this small group did on Sundays. Jeff had told me they gathered for church in a Community House, and he encouraged me to come along, so I went to see what that was like.

It was quite unimpressive. The surroundings certainly didn't help, it being a dusty, rundown house without much room for us to sit. There were some other people there whom I had not met, two deaf women. Jeff's wife Pat had to write things down for them to follow what was being said.

Another thing which I found odd was that Jeff was wearing a suit. I had not seen him in one before, and I don't think it suited him. It definitely did not fit the circumstances. A suit just looked out of place here. Overalls would have been better for where we were.

Jeff's comment about the venue was, "We could wish for better surroundings, but there again our Lord had no place to lay his head." Fair enough. It was indeed a humble meeting place, and what we did was plain and simple: we sang, we prayed, we shared the Lord's Supper, we were exhorted from God's word, and we gave money to a collection for the work of the Lord. None of that struck me as odd; none of it was new to me. What did feel odd was that there were things missing. There was no band, no organ or piano, not so much as a Jew's harp. With so few voices it sounded embarrassingly thin. The singing also lacked the zest and zing I was used to at the CRC.

Jeff kindly gave us a lift home in his little blue van, and on the way I tried to suss him out about his view on spiritual gifts. "We've been going to the CRC, but they do speak in tongues and stuff like that." He didn't respond. He suddenly looked like he was trying to concentrate intensely on the traffic. I took this as indicating a negative view of gifts of the Spirit, which was disappointing. Overall, this Sunday outing to join the small group of Christians trying to restore the teaching and practice of the New Testament church was a fizzer. I did not come away inspired and encouraged like I did when I went to their Tuesday night home study. This lot were not what I was looking for.

Soon after, I left for Sydney with my parents and a pile of books I had to read over the summer in preparation for Year 12 at Frankston High School. It was a summer of isolation from everyone I knew, bar Mum and Dad. That made it easier for me to wade through the reading I had to do. Wading through Sydney's humidity wasn't so easy.

I Learned a Lot in Year 12

My HSC year, 1981, was my first year living without my parents. I was glad to be back in Melbourne, and boarding with Mrs Wilks was a very nice deal. She didn't put any demands on me; she just made my meals and did my washing. It was five star luxury accommodation with a great cook, and the only challenge was trying to make conversation over dinner. The rest of my time was my own.

The first week of HSC was a hot one. That was typical for February. What was new to me was that I could take off after school for the Frankston Pier with one of my classmates without having to give an account to my mother. I was ahead of other classmates in my reading, so I could afford a bit of time jumping off the pier into the cooling waters of the bay. (This luxury didn't last long.)

Even though I was not yet 18 years old, I found myself in a position to make a choice concerning which church I attended — again without having to do any explaining to my parents. I soon gave the Uniting Church the flick. Nor did I return to the little church in the Community House.

I learned later that Jeff's wife, Patricia, said to him during this time, "We haven't seen Brett for a while."

"I know, I know," Jeff said. "You don't have to remind me."

But I did return — just not to their Sunday church meeting. It might have been a couple of months after coming back to Melbourne that I went along to their house on a Tuesday night. On balance, they were the most appealing group I had encountered: not part of any denomination, just Christians who were serious about learning and following God's word, more so than any other group I had found. The more time I had spent with Jeff and Pat, the more they grew on me. They were a couple who radiated the love of Christ. Their children were adorable too: well-behaved, respectful, and full of fun. When I did return on a Tuesday night they made me feel welcome; they were glad to see me again. And there were more than just the Jackmans and Pollocks now; another family of three had joined them in the meantime.

My landlady didn't go to church herself, but one Sunday when I didn't she questioned me. "Aren't you going to church today?"

"Oh, no, I've got a lot of study to do," was my excuse. I got the feeling she was disappointed that she would not get the house to herself on Sunday mornings, so that subtly encouraged me not to stick around on Sunday mornings. Being on my own, I could please myself whether I went to church or just got out of the house to give Mrs Wilks a break.

While I did not have a regular habit of going to church on Sundays for the first few months of this year, I did get into the habit of riding my bike fairly often to the Tuesday night home Bible study at the Pollocks' house. One night a man was there, sitting next to me. I didn't catch his name, but he had a moustache and receding hairline which I recognised when I met him again, years later. Roy Griffin was from New South Wales, and he got talking to me after the actual study, asking me about my faith. I can't recall what I told him, but I can remember that he kept mentioning baptism.

"I haven't been baptised," I told him, "but that's something I want to do."

"Once you're baptised, that's where it all starts," he said.

I did not understand what he meant, or why baptism was at the forefront of his thinking, but I smiled and nodded, and left it at that.

At these studies, Jeff told me in April that they had stopped meeting in the Community House and had moved their meetings to a public hall nearby. He invited me to come along and check it out, so I did. Their Sunday meetings were no longer cramped; the hall was too big for them! Their numbers had swelled, too, with about a dozen adults plus their children joining them. Most of the adults were deaf, so even with something like 20 people there, the singing still sounded thin, especially in a hall that size.

It occurred to me as we sang without any instrumental accompaniment that I might be able to help them out in that area. The hall had a piano on the stage. But I still was not certain I wanted to stay with this small group. I was still weighing them up.

Before their full assembly, they had Bible classes, and I joined one in the corner of the hall. There was a lot of background noise, because children's classes were going on in other corners of the hall. One Sunday a man in a suit, named Ivan, from somewhere else in Melbourne, was there. He joined our class, which was taught by Ben Jackman. The topic was faith: what is saving faith, according to the Bible?

During this class Ben said, "The only place in the Bible the words 'faith only' appear is in James 2:24." He had us look the verse up, and asked me to read it to the class.

I read from my golden book, "You see, then, that it is by our actions that we are put right with God, and not by our faith alone."

Ben continued, "That's the only place you'll find the words 'faith alone' or 'faith only' in the Bible, and what does it say? Faith alone cannot save you."

When Ben said that, I was sure he was wrong. "But I've seen it says somewhere that you're saved by faith alone." I had no idea where, but I was sure I had read that we are saved by faith alone.

Ivan chimed in, "Well, it might in some Bibles which translate loosely, but in the more literal translations you don't find the words 'faith only' anywhere but here in James 2." I still couldn't believe it, and they could tell. But I did not know the Bible well enough to find passages which came to mind. I had to find it later.

Ivan delivered the sermon that day, during which he said as an aside, "I saw some raised eyebrows over there when it was pointed out that 'faith only' is a term only found in James 2, where it says that you're not saved by faith only." I became all the more determined to find that place where it says we are saved by faith alone. I knew it was in there somewhere.

I never found it. I had to admit, to myself first of all, that I was mistaken. Where did I get that idea, "Saved by faith alone"? The nearest I could get was in Ephesians 2:8, but it clearly did not say we are saved by faith alone. It says, "by grace you are saved through faith". But the verse also said, "It is not the result of your own efforts"[23], so maybe that's what I was thinking of. The more likely place I got the idea was from what I had heard taught for years from my Presbyterian days until then. The idea was almost everywhere in my background, and I had never questioned it. Now I couldn't find a verse in the Bible to support it. At least, not yet. I kept looking.

I kept coming to church, too. I was learning more from the scriptures at this church than I could remember learning at any time before that. It was a feast after years of famine. Because this group were all about doing things the New Testament way, they baptised biblically: they immersed, just as I read about in the New Testament. I had not seen them baptise anyone, nor had I witnessed a baptism anywhere else. But knowing this group did it the New Testament way, I had it in mind to ask them to baptise me, for I knew I had not been baptised scripturally. One Tuesday night, after the study was finished and cuppas were being served, I sat down next to Jeff and put it to him: "I need to be baptised."

"Okay, why do you want to do that?" he asked.

"Because I was only christened in the Presbyterian Church, but in the Bible it's clear it's talking about immersion, not sprinkling."

"That's true, and I'll be happy to baptise you. But do you understand why the Bible tells us to be baptised?" he asked.

That's something I had never thought of. I didn't know what to say.

Jeff took a sheet of paper from the coffee table in front of us and said, "Okay, let's look at what Jesus said in Mark chapter 16." I found Mark 16 in my Bible. Jeff turned the page over and wrote Mark 16:16 on the blank side, so I looked at verse 16, which read, "Whoever believes and is baptized will be saved; whoever does not believe will be condemned".[24]

"According to Jesus, what do people have to do to be saved?"

---

[23] Quoted from my gold Bible ("TEV") which I was using at the time.
[24] ibid.

"Believe and be baptised," I said. That was plain enough. Jeff agreed and, next to the reference he had written on the page, he wrote:

Belief + baptism → saved

"Then look at what Peter said in Acts 2, after Jesus had returned to heaven," he continued.

I turned to Acts 2, and Jeff got me to read verse 38, which read, "Peter said to them, 'Each one of you must turn away from your sins and be baptized in the name of Jesus Christ, so that your sins will be forgiven; and you will receive God's gift, the Holy Spirit'."

This time Jeff asked me, "So what do people need to do to have their sins forgiven?"

"Repent and be baptised," I said.

"You see?" Jeff said, writing on his writing pad, "The scriptures do tell us what baptism is for."

Repent + baptised → sins forgiven

What an eye-opener! That was so plain, so obvious, I could do nothing but accept it. There was no getting around what those verses said. While I was taking all this in, with the noise and chatter of after-study refreshments going on around us, Jeff turned to another passage of scripture in his Bible. He turned the pages just like we were told not to in school, sweeping them over from half way down the edge. It was kind of painful to watch him do it. "You know about Paul's experience, what happened to him on the way to Damascus, don't you?"

"Yes."

"So after talking to Jesus, then fasting three days, Paul has Ananias visit him, and what does he say to Paul, or Saul?" he said, pointing to Acts 22:16 in his Bible. I read it in his Bible, a King James Bible, which had it as "And now why tarriest thou? arise, and be baptized, and wash away thy sins, calling on the name of the Lord."

I put what I had read in my own words: "Get baptised and wash away your sins, calling on the name of the Lord."

Jeff jotted on the page:

Baptised → sins washed away

"Well if Paul were already saved, if his sins had already been washed away when he encountered Christ on the road, or when he repented with fasting, what would Ananias have said to him?"

"Go and preach the gospel," I said without hesitation.

Jeff put his hand on my shoulder and said, "Right on, brother." It was all as plain as day, but it began to dawn on me that this meant more for me than I had realised. I had not been baptised yet. Did this mean I was not saved? Was I still lost in my sins? That did not sound right at all. It didn't make sense of all that I had been through. I could see what these scriptures said, but I needed to think and pray about this.

"Well, that's given me something to think about," I said, probably sounding bewildered.

Jeff handed the page to me. "Here you go. Give it some thought, and we can talk about it some more when you're ready."

I always went home from those Tuesday night studies having learned something new, but this week that something was really mind-blowing. There was no arguing with those passages of scripture, but there had to be more to the story. I had some searching of the scriptures to do, to see if these things were really so.[25] It couldn't be so. There had to be another explanation, and other passages of scripture were sure to reveal what that explanation was.

That night I neglected my school homework, instead looking through scriptures about baptism, and about salvation. I had a small concordance which helped me find them, and I knew most of them anyway from my previous study of the subject. But one

---

[25] cf. Acts 17:11

passage I found hit me right between the eyes. It was 1 Peter 3:21, and the part which struck me most powerfully said, "which was a symbol pointing to baptism, which now saves you." How had I not noticed this before? I wondered why Jeff had not shown me that verse, because it was as direct as you could ever want about the purpose of baptism. Baptism saves you. But how could baptism possibly save you?

There were other passages which, now that I looked at them, made it clear that until I was baptised I was not saved. Romans 6:3-5, which I had seen as so clear about the form of baptism, with its likeness to the death, burial and resurrection of Christ, had things in it which I had not noticed before. It said:

> For surely you know that when we were baptized into union with Christ Jesus, we were baptized into union with his death. By our baptism, then, we were buried with him and shared his death, in order that, just as Christ was raised from death by the glorious power of the Father, so also we might live a new life. For since we have become one with him in dying as he did, in the same way we shall be one with him by being raised to life as he was.

That said a lot. I particularly noticed that "new life" started with baptism, when we are buried with him and raised out of that grave. That obviously tied in with what Jesus called being born again, which he also called being "born of water and the Spirit."[26] I knew from that passage that I had to be born again, but now the penny had dropped that Christ put baptism squarely at the centre of that new birth.

Then there was the fact that Romans 6 says we are baptised into union with Christ and his death, and become one with him by our baptism. I knew very well if I was not one with Christ, I was still dead in my sins. This was the sense in which baptism saves us. No one can be saved from their sins without the death of Christ, and that passage was clear that baptism connected us with that death.

---

[26] John 3:3-7 (Again quoting the TEV, which I was using at the time.)

So instead of finding passages which countered what Jeff had told me, all I could find were passages that confirmed it. Later that week I talked to my girlfriend about this, and she could see this too. She was not as concerned about it as I was, but at least it confirmed I was not crazy. I just found this a hard truth to get to used to.

I went back to talk to Jeff some more about this the next weekend. We sat on the same couch in his loungeroom that afternoon, and I told him about all the other verses I had found which supported what he had told me. When I told him about 1 Peter 3:21, he said, "That was the other verse I was trying to think of, yes." I was actually glad he hadn't taken me through an exhaustive pursuit of the baptism passages. I think I needed to find them for myself, to help me accept that this was coming from God, not from some weird human thinking.

Then Jeff took me back to Acts 2:38. "What do you need to do before you are baptised, according to Peter's words?"

"Repent," I answered.

"Right. So what does that mean for you?"

"I have to stop sinning."

"Are you ever going to completely stop sinning?" he asked me.

"Unfortunately not, this side of heaven. But we all have to try."

"Right. Repentance is a change of mind, which is to produce a change of behaviour. Paul says in Acts 26:20 that we should repent and turn to God, and do works meet for repentance." He turned to the passage and read the whole verse. "Now some people have obvious things they have to change in their lives. I don't see sins in your life like drunkenness or adultery or things like that, but there are some things which God wouldn't be happy with, which you may not be aware of, so let's look at those."

He was certainly right about that, but the first thing he brought up was nothing like what I expected.

"Throughout history, when people have worshipped God, the only worship God has accepted is the worship which he ordained. So, you remember, Cain offered a sacrifice which God didn't accept. And that wasn't the last time God rejected man's efforts to worship him. Under the Old Testament, God commanded how people were to worship him, and when they did anything different, he refused to accept it. He punished people severely for it, so it shows how seriously he takes this.

"In the New Testament he commands us to do things as part of our worship to him, like pray and sing and share the Lord's Supper. You get that?"

I said I did.

"So what things have you been doing which are different to what God commands of us in the New Testament?"

This one had me stumped.

Jeff helped me. "Does God tell us to play in a band when we worship him under the New Testament?"

I offered a slow "No." The only place I could think of any mention of musical instruments was in the Old Testament. The last page of the Psalms in my Bible had an illustration of people praising the Lord with instruments. I could not think of anything like that in the New Testament.

It helped me at this point that Ben Jackman had taught a Bible class on a recent Sunday morning about the change of covenants. He had taken us through passages like Ephesians 2:14-16, Galatians 3:23-25 and Hebrews 8:8-13. I knew that we are to follow the New Testament's commands rather than the Old Testament ones; otherwise we would still be offering sheep as sacrifices.

"Is that why you don't use any instruments when you sing?" I asked.

"That's right," he said.

"I thought you just didn't have anyone who could play."

Jeff laughed briefly, then said, "So how's that sit with you?"

"Doesn't really bother me," I said. As I had already decided to change church, I was prepared for differences. I was being honest that this point was not of great concern to me anyway, although it came as a strange surprise to me. Now that I saw that they sang unaccompanied for a scriptural reason, I took it as being to their credit. They kept true to their principle of sticking to the simplicity of the Bible way. It certainly let me off the hook from having to play piano! And I didn't particularly like the sound of an organ, anyway, so I wouldn't miss that.

Jeff then raised another subject which I did not take so easily. "Something else you may not have thought about is to do with the subject of spiritual gifts. If you have a look at the scriptures, they actually speak of those gifts ceasing. Let's look at First Corinthians thirteen."

I knew the 'love chapter' well. Jeff took me to verses 8 to 13, and positioned his writing pad on the coffee table in front of us. It was clear enough that tongues were expected to cease, along with prophecies and the word of knowledge. But then he said that verse 10 indicated that this had already happened.

"Paul says those gifts would pass away when 'that which is perfect' comes. And then in verse 13 he says faith, hope and charity remain." He diagrammed this on the pad. "Think about that. When Jesus comes and we go to heaven, what do faith and hope become?"

I must have looked blank.

He continued, "Faith becomes sight. Hope is fulfilled. Romans 8 says 'Who hopes for what he sees?' So 'when that which is perfect comes' mustn't be talking about when Christ comes, because Paul says faith and hope will continue when the perfect comes. Those two things won't need to continue when Christ returns."

I could see that this made sense, but seeing what the passage doesn't mean didn't explain what it does mean. Admittedly I had a lot of my thinking invested in believing that gifts had not passed away yet, but I really could not see 1 Corinthians 13 saying *when* the gifts would pass away. Perhaps I looked unconvinced; or perhaps I looked bewildered.

Jeff continued, "To know what Paul means when he says 'that which is perfect', we have to look at what he says in verse nine. Prophecies were partial. No one prophet got the whole Bible revealed to him. Their revelations were parts of the whole picture. But Paul says in contrast to that, there will come 'that which is perfect'. The Greek word there, *teleios*, also gets translated as 'complete'. Do you see, if Paul's contrasting the partial with the complete, what that tells us about the complete, the perfect?"

"All of the prophecies put together."

"Right, the complete revelation of God's word. Paul looks ahead to when God's message to mankind is fully completed. That happened later in the first century, and we know from history that the gifts of the Spirit ceased around then too. That's the best I can do of understanding what Paul's saying in this passage."

I could see the logic, but I did not accept it. I wasn't going to argue about it, because I couldn't see any argument against what he said, except that I was certain God *was* still working miracles today, so the gifts must still be distributed today. I just said something like, "OK, I see what you mean", and thought to myself *The Spirit will get around to him; He'll change his mind.* Little did I know that the Spirit was going to work the other way — on me.

Something else Jeff wrote on the pad for me that afternoon was *tupos*. He was talking about Romans 6:17, and he wrote that because it is the Greek word for 'form' or 'pattern'. In Jeff's Bible it read, "But God be thanked, that ye were the servants of sin, but ye have obeyed from the heart that form of doctrine which was delivered you."

He was pointing out how scripture teaches that there is a recognisable "pattern of teaching"[27] which the apostles taught, and

---

27 Using the wording of the NIV & LEB from this verse.

we can and should obey it. The early disciples "were continually devoting themselves to the apostles' teaching", as part of their devotion to Christ.[28] Christ sent them out with his message, and he told them when he first authorised them, "Whoever receives you receives me."[29] He also told them, "Whatever you bind on earth shall have been bound in heaven; and whatever you loose on earth shall have been loosed in heaven."[30]

This was an important piece of teaching for me to grasp, that the apostles taught a distinct form of doctrine, and that we could discern it and obey it from the heart. I hadn't given it much thought prior to this. Jeff took me to Matthew 16:16-19, where Peter makes that pivotal declaration that Jesus is the Christ. Jesus then says specifically to Peter, "I will give the keys of the kingdom of heaven to you; and whatever you bind on earth shall have been bound in heaven, and whatever you loose on earth shall have been loosed in heaven." After looking at this, the next passage we went to was Acts 2, where Peter preached the first sermon after the cross, and announced the same thing that he had declared in Matthew 16:

> "Let all the house of Israel know assuredly that God has made this Jesus, whom you crucified, both Lord and Christ." Now having heard this, they were cut to the heart, and they said to Peter and the rest of the apostles, "Men and brothers, what shall we do?" Then Peter said to them, "Repent, and let each of you be baptized in the name of Jesus Christ for the forgiveness of sins".[31]

"What's Peter doing there?" Jeff asked me, holding a closed hand in front of him and twisting it.

I looked at the twisting motion his hand was making, and had no idea what he was hinting at. If he'd have told me how many syllables, it still wouldn't have helped.

---

[28] Acts 2:42 (NASB)

[29] Matthew 10:40 (ESV)

[30] Matthew 18:18

[31] Acts 2:36-38

"What key is he turning there?" he asked, so now I saw that he was trying to show me the motion a hand makes as it turns a key. But I still had no idea what he was talking about.

"He's been given the keys to the kingdom of heaven and he's unlocking the gate now. He's telling them how they can enter the kingdom."

"Oh. Right." I could see what he was saying now, but I really didn't see the significance of it. In time I did. Peter and the apostles were given the authority to speak on Christ's behalf about how we may please him, serve him, and be forgiven by him. It was not of their own whim, but they spoke what Christ gave them to speak, a distinctive message, a pattern of teaching which is to be obeyed.

Jeff also pointed out Jude 3, which said the faith "was once for all delivered to the saints". It did not need redelivering or repackaging today or in any other age. It had been delivered *for all*. All this was a lot to take in, all in one sitting, and I did not grasp the full implications of some things. Some of it, as I mentioned, I did not accept. Some of it was no trouble to accept. I had a lot to think about.

"That should be enough for you to take away to think about," Jeff said with his cheeky grin. He reminded me that God calls everyone to repent,[32] so a change in one's thinking is something each of us has to go through when we obey the gospel. "And when you're ready to be baptised, let me know — any time, day or night. I'll be happy to."

Acts 2:41 says that "those who gladly received his word were baptised". That definitely didn't describe me. I went away disappointed by Jeff's rejection of the Holy Spirit's gifts in our day, but I could live with that. This group were so genuine about living according to God's word, I couldn't let that one thing (which I expected God to correct in his good time) to put me off them completely. They certainly seemed to have it right on baptism, and that was something I needed to get right in my own life.

---

[32] Acts 17:30. To repent literally means to change your mind.

Tug o' War

Thinking about baptism, and what I had just learned about its importance, made me think of Jacko. My friend had decided to become a Christian, but I knew he had not been baptised. He needed to hear about this. I rang him during the week.

"Have you thought about which church you're going to join?" I asked him.

"Probably the Baptists. But I haven't done anything about it. I s'pose I should."

I had to alert him to what I had just learned. I didn't know where to start, so maybe it was best if I introduced him to Jeff. "I've found a church which just follows the Bible. They're just what I was looking for."

"Really? Where are they?"

"They have a home Bible study on Tuesday night. It's in Heatherhill Road, on the corner of Hillcrest, opposite the shops. On Sundays they're in a hall, but if you want to check 'em out, you can come along when I go on Tuesday."

"Yeah, all right," he said. That wasn't reluctance; it's just the way Jacko spoke. He actually sounded genuinely interested. He said he knew the shops, and he would probably park his motorbike outside them. Then he asked, "What's this church called?"

That was a good question. What were they called? Their notice in the local paper was just headed "Meetings". I didn't even know their name; only that they were dead serious about following the Bible, and that they were genuine Christians. I knew they were undenominational, so that's all I could tell Jacko. He would have to see for himself.

I was relieved to see Jacko roll up at the Pollocks' place on Tuesday night. There was a nagging doubt in my mind that he would come. It was good to see him anyway, as we did not catch up as often as we used to, now that he had left school. But more than that, his interest in learning about following Jesus gave us something in common beyond friendship.

Jacko came away from the study as impressed as I was when I first attended. The excellent teaching, the lovely people, it all made for a great experience of Christian fellowship. Before he left, he asked where they met on Sunday, and I explained when and where to go, and he rode off into the night. I was stoked. Roll on, Sunday!

I had taken Jacko along to the CRC before, so he was used to a loud and lively event with an amplified band, clapping, hands in the air, and of course a session of harmonic gibberish. He had a bemused look of distaste when they took up a collection, joyfully singing, "He that giveth liberally shall be blessed abundantly." It was shamelessly mercenary.

There was none of that on Sunday, with this lot. It was about as plain and simple as church could get, and I think Jacko felt a lot more comfortable with it. He didn't say a lot, but what he said was positive. He liked the people, too. You couldn't *not* like the people. When we had a chance afterwards, we asked Jeff what the name of the church is.

Jeff looked pleased with the question. "We don't actually have a name. In the New Testament, you see the church called a number of different things, mostly just 'the church', and we're fine with any of those descriptions. We've been discussing what's best to put in our ads, so that people can see who we are. It's not easy, because we don't want people to mistake us for one of the denominations. We just want to be the Lord's church, but how you get that across is the question. We like 'church of Christ', but so people don't think we're the 'Frankston Church of Christ', we've gone with 'Bay City church of Christ' at this stage."

Jacko asked, "When you say denominations, and undenominational, what does all that mean?" Jacko and Jeff both had English accents, but they were different accents.

"Well, we don't have any organisational ties to any other congregation. Denominations typically have a hierarchy with a governing body, Popes, archbishops and what have you. They draw up creeds and often go by some name that they've come up with themselves. But you don't see that in the New Testament. In the first century, they were subject to Christ, you see. Denominations end up with a whole range of unbiblical practices, and we don't want to go down that road."

I could see the difference, having been in the Uniting Church, with its synods and President and so on. Jacko didn't have anything to compare from his unchurched background. He looked at me, perhaps expecting me to have something to say.

"So you're non-denominational, not inter-denominational," I offered.

"Yes," Jeff confirmed.

"What's the difference?" Jacko asked.

I left this to Jeff. "Inter-denominational means you don't care so much about the differences in doctrine and practice, and what denomination you attend. Non-denominationalism holds that denominations are unbiblical, and we should just be Christians without all these brand names and human creeds and traditions."[33]

"Fair enough," Jacko said.

Before we left, we went over to a tract rack they had near the door, and Jacko took a handful of different tracts. (I had already raided this rack previously, and had a collection at home.) Most of them were a series of short tracts with a big question mark on the front of each, one called "What is Salvation?", others "What is Faith?" "What is Repentance?" "What is Baptism?" and "What is the Church?" All that was in these tracts was a series of questions, answered by direct quotations of scripture. Jacko had plenty of reading to do.

During the week, Jacko dropped into my place to talk on his way

---

[33] Bear in mind that this was in 1981. Since then, this distinction has been blurred to the point where "non-denominational" is commonly used to mean something completely different to what it used to mean.

home one afternoon. I brought him into my room, away from Mrs Wilks' hearing, and we discussed at length the things we had been reading, and our impressions of this new little undenominational congregation. We agreed that the idea that baptism was required in order to be saved was a big step outside what we had previously thought. But I was more convinced than Jacko. He had been talking to Rick, our school friend who was a Baptist, and Rick was stridently against baptism having anything to do with salvation.

"Rick kept saying 'we're saved by faith', and if you read John 3:16 it says all you have to do is believe."

"But did he mean we're saved by faith alone?" I asked. "Because I haven't been able to find anywhere that says you're saved by faith alone; only a verse that says we're not."

"Really?"

"Yeah, in James 2."

"Show me that. I want to see that," Jacko said with genuine eagerness. "What does it say?"

We looked it up and found verse 24. "Whoa, that's pretty clear!" Jacko said.

I also took him to those other passages which clearly show that baptism is not just a nice gesture, but that it serves an important role in our getting our sins forgiven.

"Well, yeah…I dunno," he said slowly and thoughtfully, after we had spent some time examining the scriptures. "I'll have to think about all that."

"It's not what I've been used to, but I can see it's what the scriptures say," I said. "It actually makes sense of baptism."

"What, getting pushed under water like a drowned rat to become a Christian?" Jacko laughed. I had to laugh too. Our time had run out and dinnertime was upon us, so Jacko headed home for his.

The following Saturday Jacko came to my place with another tract —
a Baptist one. He had been to see Rick, and Rick was determined to
straighten Jacko out on this. I had a look at the tract, and it argued
at length about why it could not be true that baptism had any
connection with our salvation. It said that baptism was merely a
testimony of what Christ had already done for us; he had saved us,
and we were to be baptised to show that. It was "an outward sign of
an inward grace".

The tract argued very persuasively; there was no denying that. I
knew what was different about it. "I can see what this is saying, but
it goes on with a lot of argument to try and prove its point. But," I
said, pointing to the question mark tracts, "these tracts just quote
scripture."

Jacko's face showed he recognised the contrast. "Yeah, you're right.
If it's true, you should be able to see it in the Bible."

I felt like I was getting somewhere with Jacko. We decided to ride
our bikes — mine being a pushbike — down to Rick's house to talk to
him about this. I was confident that he would see what I could see
in the scriptures. Jacko knew where Rick lived, but I had never been
there. We found him at home and he invited us into his room. He
was listening to a record called "Hooked on Classics," which took
classical music and put a disco beat to it. "That's musical
blasphemy!" I declared. Rick was such an intensely serious fellow, I
couldn't resist stirring him.

He was intensely serious about doctrine, too, and that was a good
thing. But when you had a different view to Rick, he was positively
intimidating. I really felt like I was locking horns with someone,
rather than searching the scriptures together. He argued that
nothing could add to Christ's saving work on the cross; I certainly
didn't dispute that. He cited passages which spoke of belief in
connection with salvation, but which did not mention baptism. I
likewise didn't dispute them, but most of the verses didn't mention
confession or repentance either.

When we talked about John 3, he pointed out verses 15 to 18, where
the word "believe" appears five times, and he said that verse 16 is

universally recognised as the most important verse in the Bible. I remembered that my little red Gideon's Bible had John 3:16 in about 20 different languages at the front, so I understood what he meant there. But I had to draw attention to the context in which that verse sat. At the start of the chapter, Jesus spoke of being born again, being born of water and the Spirit.

"That's not talking about baptism," he countered.

"Well what *is* it talking about?" I asked.

"Jesus is talking about our physical birth and our spiritual birth. When we were born as babies, there was water — water comes out of the mother, too. But when we're born again, that's a spiritual birth. That's all Jesus is saying there."

That was a new take (to me) on being born of water and the Spirit. "So you take that bit about water as talking about the placental juices when you're born?" (At 17, I didn't know they were actually called amniotic fluid.)

"Yes," Rick affirmed.

This seemed so far-fetched, I didn't know what to say about it. Would Jesus really have to teach Nicodemus that to enter the kingdom of God, you had to be born in the first place?

About this time, a friend of Rick's showed up. I think I had met him before, at the Baptist church. Rick told him that we were having a discussion about baptism, whether one had to be baptised to be saved.

"Oh, no," his friend said confidently, shaking his head. It was as though they'd had this drummed into them, so that any consideration of the question was ruled out. I could see I was getting outnumbered by Baptists, so I did not want to continue the discussion. But before I left they brought up an interesting case: the thief on the cross.[34] Jesus didn't require *him* to be baptised, yet he

---

[34] Luke 23:39-43 (compare Matthew 27:44)

promised him he would be in Paradise that very day. This was a fair point to consider. It was not the last time I encountered people appealing to this famous thief. In fact, his conversion seems to be more celebrated than Saul's or the three thousand at Pentecost, in some circles.

I'm actually not sure what I said about the thief when they brought him up. I think I'd given up by this stage, but I do know that I could see the uniqueness of the thief's situation, hanging as he was right next to the Son of God, who had "authority on earth to forgive sins".[35] Jesus went around telling a lot of people their sins were forgiven. But today, after the cross, he's not walking around "on earth" in the flesh, telling people that their sins are forgiven. Before he left the earth, he told the apostles how people could be saved "until the end of the age", and sent them out to spread that good news.[36]

It was obvious our disagreement was not getting resolved, and I moved on to talking about the musical blasphemy that was playing, before getting around to saying I was going. Jacko left with me, and Rick offered us some further exhortations to accept his point of view.

Out on the street, with our bikes, Jacko and I briefly chatted before parting.

"You certainly got him worked up," he said to me with a smile.

"Yeah, I couldn't believe some of the things he was saying."

Looking back, I see Jacko must have felt like he was right in the middle in a tug of war. I really wanted him to accept what I had just learned, and Rick wanted the opposite. It can't have been easy for him.

---

[35] Luke 5:21-24

[36] Matthew 28:18-20; Mark 16:15-16; Luke 24:46-47

I Surrender All

I didn't want to chase and badger Jacko, so I let him mull on things for a while. So did I. June came, and I still had not been baptised. I had not realised it, but I was actually waiting for Jacko to make the decision to be baptised. Then we could do it together. But I was sitting up in bed one night, reading a passage of scripture which spoke of the good things God's children have in Christ. It suddenly occurred to me that none of what I was reading applied to me, because I had not been born again. The letter was written to people in Christ, and I had not been baptised into Christ,[37] baptised into his death,[38] so I was still on the outside, looking in. The gravity of my spiritual state had dawned on me at last.

I know it was silly of me to delay any longer, but I had my close friend on my mind, and I was intent on convincing him of what I had come to believe. The following Sunday at church, somewhere in the sermon, Jeff quoted what Jesus said in John 15:5. "Apart from me you can do nothing." Those words sank heavily into me. Here was I trying to convince Jacko and anybody else who would listen, that we must be born of water and the Spirit—and all the time I was carrying on apart from Christ.

I went home, and after lunch I rang Jacko. He hadn't been at church for a few weeks. I had to know what he was thinking. "What do you think you'll do?" I asked him.

He sounded uncomfortable as he replied, "I think —" He cleared his throat. "I know you won't like this, but I think I'm gunna go with Rick's church."

To be honest, I don't know what I said after that. I just know I tried not to show how disappointed I was. After our conversation, walking back through the house to my bedroom, I felt a heavy aloneness. I was apart from Christ, and also on my own in seeing the need to be baptised into him. I went back to my room and took stock of my situation. This was when I realised that I had been

---

[37] Galatians 3:27

[38] Romans 6:3-4

putting off submitting to Christ in baptism until Jacko was ready to do it. (Stupid, I know.) But now he had been turned off the idea, I really had no reason to delay any longer. What did Ananias say to Paul? "And now why are you waiting? Arise and be baptized, and wash away your sins."[39]

I got on the phone to ring Jeff. There was no answer. Then I remembered that he had said that his family and the Jackmans were going to visit a church somewhere closer to Melbourne that night. They must have already left, and that meant I would not have a chance to see them until after dinner — after dark.

Thinking this through, I knew very well what my landlady would think of my going out after dark on a wet winter's night to get baptised. She had already, without speaking to me about it, written letters of concern to my parents about my not keeping my room as tidy as I should, and having smelly socks. She would probably freak out and get on the phone to Sydney straightaway if I said, "I'll be back later, Mrs Wilks. I'm just popping out to get baptised." I knew I had to wait until she went to bed, then slip out the back way.

It was raining and windy as I planned this. I really picked a great night for it. I had to pack my school bag with a change of clothes. While I let time pass, I got some homework done while Mrs Wilks watched the telly. The rain eased off, but the wind kept up. The wind would help me get out without being heard, so that was a good thing.

The landlady's well-meaning Labrador, Ella, could be a complication. She slept on the couch in the TV room at night. Whenever I got home late and crept through the house, Ella's tail would wag, thumping the couch or whatever it happened to be near. There was no way I could sneak through the house undetected. My plan was to go out my bedroom window door, through the back courtyard to the garage, where my bike was. There was a gate from the yard to a park behind the property. This gate was at the far

---

[39] Acts 22:16 (NKJV)

corner of the block from my landlady's bedroom, so getting out that way was going to cause no problems.

Half an hour after Mrs Wilks had retired to her bedroom, I made my move. I rugged myself up against the cold, wrapping my long green scarf around my neck. As I got out my door and across the courtyard under the cover of darkness and the wind, I was thankful the rain had stopped. With my bag secured in the pack-rack of my bike, I got off the property and into the park. When I was far enough away not to be heard, I mounted my trusty Repco treadley and was away through dark, wet streets.

It took about 15 minutes to get over to the Pollocks' house, with quiet roads and the wind pushing me around a bit. The knot in my chest grew tighter as I neared my destination. When I opened their gate and brought my bike into the yard, I was relieved to see a light still on in the house.

Jeff answered my knock on their front door, saying "Hello" with a look and tone which said, *what are you doing knocking on my door at this time?* I found out later that he didn't recognise me at first, I was so rugged up.

"You're gunna kill me for this," I said.

"Oh! Come in."

I stepped in, carrying my white schoolbag. "I tried to ring you earlier, but you were out, so I had to wait till my landlady went to bed."

"So, what's on your mind?" he asked me as I sat down.

I didn't say the 'B' word, and I don't know why. "It's time I took the plunge."

"Why now?"

"I just have to do it."

"That's fair enough. There's no reason to wait once you've decided to do it. Where would you like to do it? One of the members has a pool in their backyard, or we can go to the beach."

"I think I'd rather do it at the beach."

"Yes, the sea's good. I like it," he said. "I'll just ring Ben and let him know." He picked up the phone and was soon speaking. "Hullo-ee. Brett's come around, and he'd like to be baptised."

There. He said it. When I heard the word 'baptised', the enormity of the occasion struck me. This was it. It had taken me ages to get here, but I was going to be baptised into Christ this very night.

When Jeff hung up the phone, he turned to me and said, "Well, you certainly picked the biblical hour!" I did not follow what he meant, but later I twigged that he was alluding to Acts 16:33, where the Philippian prison keeper and his family were baptised in the middle of the night. At least in my case it wasn't after midnight!

Pat came into the loungeroom, giving me her usual warm greeting, and Jeff told her why I was there. "Oh, wonderful news!" she said, and added with a light laugh, "You picked a good night for it. Where will you do it?" she asked Jeff.

"We'll just go to the beach," Jeff said, sitting down next to me with his Bible. We were soon engaged in some more discussion of what the Bible said about surrendering to Jesus. Jeff talked about what it meant to confess Jesus as 'Lord'. "You understand that this means you give up your own rights. From now on, whatever Jesus says, goes. Your life will belong to him."

"Yes," I calmly said. This was exciting! But I remained calm on the outside.

While we were waiting for Ben to arrive, Jeff explained what he would do as he baptised me. He was going to lay me backwards into the water, so I should hold my nose with one hand, and his arm with the other, bending my knees as I went backwards. I had never seen a baptism before, so I was glad he took the time to explain how he was going to do it.

Ben soon arrived. He was to be our driver. As we got up to go, Pat came with us to the door and said with her hand on my shoulder, "See you when you get back, a new creature!"[40]

It was about 10:20pm when we pulled up in an empty car park between Frankston Pier and Kananook Creek. The waves were foaming noisily in the wind as Jeff and I dispensed with our shoes and jackets. We waded our way to deep enough water, with waves breaking against us, and got into position. As he pushed me under, a wave came through and my feet left the ground and floated up a bit. That wasn't supposed to happen, and afterwards I asked Jeff whether I was fully immersed. "Don't worry about that: *I* was nearly fully immersed myself, with that wave washing over us!"

As we waded back towards shore, a flash went off. Ben had brought his camera. I was especially glad he brought a large blanket which he wrapped around me when I reached him on the beach. That was it. There was no crowd, no fanfare or applause. Just the wind and the waves rejoicing.

> *I was in the mud, the night was dark*
> *When I felt your hand on my soul*
> *You helped me stand, you led the way*
> *And I followed you in from the cold*
>
> *The light you spoke revealed my mud*
> *And put all my blackness to shame*
> *But you were warm, and the night was wet*
> *So I followed you in from the rain*
>
> *My clothes of mud you washed in blood*
> *And buried in the watery grave*
> *My sins were purged and I emerged*
> *A new child, blessed and saved* [41]

---

[40] 2 Corinthians 5:17; Romans 6:4-6

[41] A poem I attempted not long afterwards. I later scrawled next to it, "sing-song trash", but it does capture how I felt at the time. I do think American songwriter Mickey Cates did a much nicer job years later in his beautiful song, "Baptism".

The Week Goes On

Jeff dropped me next to the park, and we got my bike out of the back of his van. I had showered and changed at his place, and left my wet clothes there. (There was no way I was going to risk explaining to Mrs Wilks how my shirt and jeans had been saturated with salt water overnight.) I made it back into the house without detection, got into bed and went to sleep to the silent sound of angels singing in celebration.

Monday morning was like walking through a dream with my feet off the ground. (After all that praying about levitating, it finally happened!) With the world behind me and the cross before me, I was determined never to sin again.

I told a few of my classmates that I had been baptised the night before, and they voiced their approval. One was a Mormon, a couple Baptists, and one was a mate of Jacko who was now also a mate of mine. Mark had shown enough interest in our religious involvement that he came to church a few times. When I told him in our Legal Studies class about what I had done the night before, he asked me a bunch of questions.

"Did you feel lifted spiritually? Does it feel like a burden has been lifted from your shoulders?" He seemed to view it as something emotional, something subjective. Sure there was the emotional buzz, and maybe he saw it in me that Monday. But I had made the decision to be baptised into Christ after a lot of careful, prayerful consideration of the facts. It was a reasoned process from studying the scriptures.

After school I rang Jacko and asked him to come over after tea, because I had something important to tell him. I didn't want to tell him on the phone where my landlady might overhear, but he may have guessed what it was. When he came, I took him into my room, where I could tell him all.

"Wow, you must've really meant it." He was probably thinking about the weather the night before. It was amazing how much more receptive he was, now that I was telling him what I had done. It was no longer a hypothetical idea; I had been born again. The fact that I had to sneak out at night just added amusement to it all.

I explained what had convinced me, showing him scriptures like Acts 22:16. "I mean, what else could 'wash away your sins' mean? Paul already believed, because he'd seen Jesus. Obviously he'd already repented, 'cause he was fasting. But Ananias still tells him to get up and be baptised and wash away his sins! He still hadn't had his sins washed away, and you can see why when you look at Romans 6. That's where it says we're baptised into Christ's death, so you haven't connected with the blood of Jesus till you've been baptised — and without Christ's death, without his blood you can't be forgiven.

"It all fits together and makes sense of verses like Acts 2:38 and Mark 16:16. They say our sins are forgiven when we repent and are baptised, and those who believe and are baptised will be saved."

I don't know how long I went on, but Jacko listened to it all, offering positive comments. It was like I had earned the right to be heard by going ahead and doing what God commanded. The power of example had given weight to my words. I could see he was pleased for me, and as he left he said, "Well done" and "Good on you." I took that as a positive sign. He wasn't a lost cause yet.

My girlfriend, however, was. The following day she showed up at lunchtime and we had lunch in the park opposite the school gate. When I told her that I was baptised on Sunday night, her reaction was, "Why didn't you ring me?" There was not the slightest hint that she thought anything positive about it. I don't know why she didn't dump me straight away, because it was obvious she didn't care about Christianity anymore. Why didn't I walk away from the relationship straight away? Like the Chicago song said a few years later, she was "a hard habit to break."

But the day I told her I had been born again, all the signs were there that our relationship was heading for the rocks. I walked back into the school grounds unwilling to acknowledge those signs. But I think I knew in my heart of hearts that our days were numbered.

That was Tuesday. I didn't go to the Bible Study that night, but I cannot remember why. Surely homework wouldn't keep me, but perhaps it did. Year 12 did have its demands. Or maybe it was pouring with rain, so I could not ride over. Whatever the reason, Tuesday was totally overshadowed by Wednesday.

After tea on Wednesday night, from my bedroom I heard Mrs Wilks answer the front door, and soon I heard Jacko's voice. I got up and he met me at my bedroom door as I came out of it. (He told me later that he had all but pushed his way past Mrs Wilks as he barged in to get to me.)

"Come on, mate," he said, "We're going to the beach."

"The beach?"

"Yep. Jeff and Ben are waiting in the car."

"Oh! Just a minute, I'll grab my jacket."

As Jacko and I made our way to the front door, I said to Mrs Wilks, "I've just got to go out for a bit. I won't be long, I don't think."

"Oh, okay," she said. Poor thing. There was nothing she could say or do about it, really. But this was sure to make it into her next letter to my parents.

We went to the same place as three of us had gone on Sunday night. We were earlier this night, but it was still cold. I got the job of holding the blanket ready for when the new creature emerged from the dark waves. The four of us were back into Ben's little white sedan as soon as we could, and soon Jeff starting singing *I Have Decided to Follow Jesus*. I joined in, but I knew a slightly different tune, so I wasn't much help.

Back at the Pollocks' place, Jacko headed for the bathroom to shower, getting a hug from Pat on the way. Pat had mended a hole in one of Jacko's motorbike gloves while he was out getting into Christ. "I wanted to do something for my new brother," she brightly said. She was such a Christlike gem!

After talking with me on Monday night, Jacko had gone to the Tuesday night study and spoke to Jeff afterwards, asking questions about baptism. He was back there the following night with a change of clothes. Despite all the persistent attempts to dissuade him from doing what the scriptures command, Jacko had decided to follow Jesus. So had I. It was a great week.

The Newborns Grow

The people at church on Sunday were obviously thrilled, greeting me as soon as I walked into the hall. They all knew about what had happened in the past week. It was a tad too much attention for my liking, but Jacko didn't seem to mind. I quickly learned from the deaf members how to sign "baptised", and my quote for the day had to do with the lesson I had learned: "Apart from me, you can do nothing".

That chap Roy Griffin, whoever he was, had it right: baptism was just the beginning. Jacko and I had a great time learning everything we could in the months that followed. Some things I learned were quite baffling at first, simply because I had been used to believing some unbiblical doctrines for long enough to consider them unquestionable truth…only to find that they could not be supported by scripture. I knew that God's word is truth[42] — no question about that — but our understanding of God's word is something we should be willing to question and re-examine. "Truth fears no investigation" was a saying I learned from Jeff.

But the first thing I had to come to grips with in my new life was my failure to remain sinless. As I said earlier, I had resolved never to sin again. I knew what Romans 6:11-14 said:

> Likewise you also, consider yourselves to be dead indeed to sin, but alive to God in Christ Jesus our Lord. Therefore do not let sin reign in your mortal body, that you should obey it in its lusts, nor present your members as instruments of unrighteousness to sin, but present yourselves to God as being alive from the dead, and your members as instruments of righteousness to God. For sin shall not be master over you, for you are not under law but under grace.

So, as far as I was concerned, I was finished with sin. It was a thing of my past. It wasn't long until I realised, following my baptism, that I had failed to keep from sinning, and when I did, I was

---

[42] John 17:17; Psalm 119:160

shattered. I had blown it without even thinking about it. Even though I knew what the scriptures say about the forgiveness and cleansing that is in Christ,[43] and that our own righteousness is "like filthy rags",[44] I still found it crushing that I couldn't keep from sinning. I was a walking case of Romans 7, as every Christian is.

Coming to terms with my own ongoing sinfulness, and learning to accept God's grace and ongoing forgiveness, was my first big lesson after being born again. That last sentence in the quote (above) from Romans 6 was something I took some time to absorb. Having been baptised into Christ, I was "not under law but under grace", so sin could no longer send me down the chute to damnation. It no longer had mastery over me like it used to, so whenever I stumbled (and "we all stumble in many ways"[45]) I could get up and keep walking in the light, cleansed by the blood of Christ. My self-condemnation was ill-founded, for there is "now **no condemnation** for those who are in Christ Jesus"![46] I could now thumb my nose at sin, which was no longer my master, and walk away from it.

Other less personally difficult lessons came my way, too. In my reading of books and tracts (which took considerable time away from my school studies) I came across a statement that stunned me: Nowhere in scripture does it say that Christ will ever set foot on the earth again. *What?* Once again I set about finding that verse which I was sure I had seen...but which I couldn't find. Acts 1:11 was the closest I could get, but that did not show decisively that Jesus would set foot on the ground, only that he would come back.

I soon found I had to "unlearn" the messy, mixed up beliefs I had picked up from end-times theorists like Hal Lindsey and most of my friends right back to my Presbyterian days. It took months to turn my thinking around to grasp the simple teaching of scripture, because my thinking was so saturated with premillennial ideas. Whole slabs of scripture which I thought were talking about our

---

[43] Ephesians 1:7-8; 1 John 1:7-10

[44] Isaiah 64:6 (NKJV)

[45] James 3:2

[46] Romans 8:1

generation turned out to be actually talking about things which had happened long ago. It's easy to see — unless you've been steeped in reading some other meaning into the passages. So it wasn't easy for me to get used to, but as I studied those passages they began to make a whole lot more sense than they had. It was actually astounding to see the accuracy of fulfilled prophecies in history.

As my faith in God's word grew, I learned to trust what he said over what the majority of the religious world said, and over what I had been used to thinking. To quote a car sticker of that day, "God said it. I believe it. That settles it." I realised that the majority was definitely not a safe guide for ascertaining the truth. Christ's words in Matthew 7:13-14 were particularly pertinent:

> Enter by the narrow gate. For the gate is wide and the way
> is easy that leads to destruction, and those who enter by it
> are many. For the gate is narrow and the way is hard that
> leads to life, and those who find it are few.

In our elation at having learned the truth, being set free,[47] Jacko and I found that other people we knew did not share our excitement. We already expected that our friends who had entrenched doctrinal positions would not be pleased with our conversions. And it was no big shock to us that those who were antagonistic to Christ and his message did not share our joy. But it was perplexing when people we thought shared our love for truth[48] did not share our enthusiasm when we exclaimed, "Eureka! Look what we've found!" Truth-seekers don't mind too much when they find out they've been wrong on something, because any disappointment is outweighed by the thrill of learning the truth. That's how I felt, and I expected others who professed a love for truth to share that sentiment.

That year, Keith Green published an article in his *Last Days Newsletter* called, "What's Wrong with the Gospel?" I've already said that I hung on every word Keith Green said, and this was one article which resonated with me, highlighting how modern religion

---

[47] John 8:31-32

[48] 2 Thessalonians 2:10b

has robbed the gospel of its essence. Now I found that the article fell short in a big way: it didn't point out the things which I had just learned—things essential to the gospel, of which I had been blissfully unaware.

During the same period, *The Last Days Newsletter* ran a series of articles about the Catholic Church, exposés on where that religion had gone wrong. While it was very informative, the big point left undealt with (or even acknowledged) was that there were a whole lot of other denominations out there, and they each had their own set of problems. Catholics were not alone in straying from the truth. I decided to write to Keith. I felt like we were kindred spirits in our love for the truth. I got Jacko on board with this. In two letters in one, we shared with Keith, in our own clumsy new-convert way, what we had learned. It was a heavy disappointment that we received no acknowledgement, either directly or in the *Letters to the Editor* column. I was naïvely sure we would have a better response than we were getting from people we knew. I didn't bother renewing my subscription.

The truth about the Holy Spirit and his gifts was something I took most of two years to get my head around. One reason was there was a lot of confusion about it even amongst those in the Lord's church. Jeff left me to wrestle with it for myself, providing only a counter-point sounding board when I brought ideas to bounce off him. The cessation of the gifts of the Spirit was the easy part, once I learned to accept what God said as supreme over all human opinions and experiences. It was how the scriptures' teaching on the whole subject fit together, and what that meant for us today, that took much longer to sort out.[49] With the background I came from, I had to resolve this one properly to settle my mind on it. The shallow and inept interpretations I started with would not do, and I knew God's word must have the answers.

---

[49] I published the results of my studies in 2002, in *The Spirit of Truth ~ Truth of the Spirit*, so I won't detail this at length here. I say a bit more about it in the Appendix to this book.

There were lots of things I had to let go and leave behind when I came into the body of Christ—even some people. The song *I Have Decided to Follow Jesus* puts it well when it says, "Though few go with me, still I will follow" and "The world behind me, the cross before me." It wasn't that I rejected people, but they rejected me when they saw I was seeking first the kingdom of God and his righteousness. It was a cost I had counted, and was willing to pay. My family were far from happy to learn that I had stepped out of the institutionalised religious world and into "some tin-pot church" (to use my mother's words). It was very hard for them to conceive of the idea of just being a Christian without being a part of a denomination.

My girlfriend came to church now and then, but she grew increasingly cold as weeks passed. The last time she came was a couple of months after I was baptised into Christ. On that day, after the more organised bits were finished, I was talking with members there and she said she'd go to the shops and I could catch up with her there. Clearly I wasn't quick enough to go and catch up, because she came back and I was still engrossed in conversation with Ben. (Did time fly, or did she?) I wrapped up the conversation and walked out with her. Blind Freddy could see that being with God's people was a higher priority for me than being with her. She could see it, for sure. Walking away from the hall together, as soon as I uttered a word—"Sorry"—she snarled the all-too-common, caustic two-word curse at me with such venom and volume that I was sure members in the hall heard it. I heard her loud and clear, and it wasn't long till that horrible relationship was over. It was difficult to put it behind me, but what a blessing it was to finally do it!

The religious friends I had at school, and back in Aspendale, soon cooled off as they saw I had turned my back on institutionalised religion—in other words, their religious world. My "new convert zeal" was not matched by sufficient wisdom and knowledge in the scriptures to be very effective at explaining the way of God more accurately to them.[50] (I must admit that coming up with the saying "denominations are abominations" didn't help me keep friends and

---

[50] Acts 18:26

influence people, and I learned not to say it after the first few times!) And it is fair to say that most of the people I knew were happy where they were, religiously, so I really should not have expected them to be receptive to the concept of the New Testament Way.

The rejection I experienced from friends and loved ones was both disheartening and frustrating. What made it easier was knowing that it was all for the sake of my decision to follow Jesus, who was worth more than anything or anyone else in the world. I had found "a pearl of great value", and nothing was worth more to me.[51] Learning what I was from God's word, I was experiencing what Jesus spoke of in John 8:31-32, when he said, "If you continue in my word, truly you are my disciples. And you shall know the truth, and the truth shall set you free." It really was exhilarating to be learning the truth, and it still is — because I am still learning and growing, decades later.

Another thing which made it easier to leave the world behind me was coming to know and love all the wonderful people I met in this family of believers. This is also something Jesus anticipated in an exchange with Peter:

> Then Peter began to say to Him, "See, we have left all things and have followed you."
>
> So Jesus answered and said, "Assuredly, I say to you, there is no one who has left house or brothers or sisters or father or mother or wife or children or fields, for my sake and for the sake of the gospel, who shall not receive a hundredfold now in this time — houses and brothers and sisters and mothers and children and fields, along with persecutions — and in the age to come, eternal life.[52]

The believers I have come to know and love are, of course, too many to speak of here, but one lady I met six months after I was born again was Janie Penfold, a woman not much older than my mother.

---

[51] Matthew 13:45-46

[52] Mark 10:28-30

After my school year was finished,[53] I went to Sydney to stay with my parents, and while I was there, Jacko and I attended a camp northwest of Sydney. Despite the discomfort of tenting in primitive and humid conditions, it was a thrill to meet a whole mixed bag of loving, devoted New Testament Christians. Janie asked me about how I found the Lord, and I told her in a nutshell. (I couldn't convey all the circumstances which combined to bring about my conversion; just what had happened to bring me into contact with the Pollocks.)

"It really is amazing how God worked it, when I think about it," I said. "If my family hadn't have moved to Frankston for those couple of years, and if the Pollocks hadn't have moved there during that time and started those home meetings—"

"He'd have got to you another way," Janie chimed in.

"Really? You think so?"

"Oh, I *know* so—definitely," she said, with the assurance of someone who had many more years walking with God than I.

In time I learned why Janie believed that. The scriptures reveal a God who is at work in the lives of people everywhere, helping those who love the truth and seek him. One verse from Hebrews 11 will suffice to sum this up here:

> But without faith it is impossible to please him, for he who comes to God must believe that he is, and that he is a rewarder of those who diligently seek him.

---

[53] Incidentally, I obtained my HSC, even though I gave so much time to extracurricular studies. Matthew 6:33 in action!

Are We There Yet?

"Do you ever question whether you've joined the wrong church?" John asked me. We were alone in the kitchen of the hall where my congregation met, and I think he was asking me because we had both become Christians around the same time, but we only met months later.

"Oh, sure," I replied without hesitation. "I question it all the time. I keep looking for something in scripture that I've missed which'll show that I've got it wrong. But I haven't found anything."

I knew what John meant, so I answered his question, a question which came because his relatives were constantly telling him he had "joined the wrong church". But really, he and I did not join a church. When we surrendered to the Lord in being "baptised into one body",[54] the Lord added us to *his* church.[55] We didn't have to go choosing a church to join. We just chose Jesus, and being united with him put us into his body. After that, it's just a matter of finding others in the body (if we haven't already) and joining them.[56]

But finding ourselves in the body of Christ, the one body of all those whom God has purchased with his own blood,[57] that is not the end of the journey. That's what Roy Griffin was talking about, and what the apostle Paul acknowledged in Philippians 3:12-15, when he said:

> Not that I have already obtained, or have already been made perfect; but I press on, if also I may lay hold of that for which I was laid hold of by Christ Jesus. Brothers, I do not count myself to have laid hold; but one thing I do, forgetting those things which are behind, and reaching forward to those things which are ahead, I press toward the goal for the prize of the upward call of God in Christ Jesus.

---

[54] 1 Corinthians 12:13

[55] Acts 2:41, 47

[56] Acts 9:26; 21:4

[57] Acts 20:28

> Therefore, as many as are mature, let us think this way; and
> if in anything you think otherwise, even this God will
> reveal to you.

I've learned that one of Satan's dirtiest tricks (because it helps so many seekers get lost) is to persuade us that our journey is over, that we've arrived. If we think that, we'll stop seeking. If we stop seeking, we stop growing — growing closer to the Lord, growing "in the grace and knowledge of our Lord and Saviour Jesus Christ."[58] The scriptures tell us this, but my own experience also taught it to me. If I had stopped seeking, if I had stopping asking questions earlier on, I would never have come into contact with the saving blood of Jesus, into Christ, where redemption and forgiveness of sins is found.[59]

One thing my journey of faith has taught me is that we each should never buy Satan's lie that we have arrived. And we should never forget that others are on the same journey. Some are further along the road than we are, and we can learn from their experience. But thinking about my own journey reminds me that there are many who are further back on the road to God, where I once was, and I can help them. I can offer some advice, and explain the way of God more accurately to them. That's why I was happy to find Tran and Greg (the door-knockers I told you about at the start) at my door, and invited them in. They are on a journey of faith, just like I am. Coming from where I did on this journey, I can relate very much to where they are now. Fellow travellers can help each other,[60] if we are willing to open the scriptures to see what God says, and let God have the last word.

**"YOU SHALL KNOW THE TRUTH
AND THE TRUTH SHALL SET YOU FREE."**

---

58 2 Peter 3:18

59 Ephesians 1:7

60 Proverbs 27:17

Appendix

Some who have read this story have said they wished I'd expanded on some of the points of doctrine I had touched on in the narrative. Rather than go back and insert them at the risk of losing the flow of thought, this Appendix gives some brief explanations of things in which I learned "the way of God more accurately" (Acts 18:26).

Change of Covenants

In all my time around church people, hearing sermons and Bible readings, I never learned about the change of covenants, and the differences between the old and new covenants. I would hear it read that Jesus said, "This cup is the new covenant in my blood"—and I had no idea what he meant. "New covenant"? What was the old covenant?

It turns out this was a very basic thing to understand if you want to make sense of the scriptures. There's two main parts to the Bible: Old Testament and New Testament. In current-day Bibles, the word "covenant" is usually used instead of "testament". Hebrews is the biggest resource for learning about the change of covenants, but it's a tough read. Maybe that's why I hadn't grasped this, but it's full of statements like this:

> He takes away the first in order that he may establish the second.

> For if that first covenant had been faultless, then no place would have been sought for a second.

> He is also mediator of a better covenant, which has been enacted upon better promises.

> But you have come…to Jesus, the mediator of a new covenant.

It made it a whole lot easier to understand what God expects of us when I came to understand that Jesus "abolished in his flesh the enmity, that is, the law of commandments contained in ordinances" (Eph 2:15), and that "the law has become our custodian, leading us to Christ, so that we might be justified by faith. But after faith has come, we are no longer under a custodian" (Gal 3:24-25). So in learning how to please God, I had to bear in mind that the Old Testament scriptures were not the guide; they pointed to One who is the guide. I had to look to what commands Jesus gave his apostles to take to the world after his resurrection (Matt 28:18-20; Acts 2:42).

While the Old Testament is no longer binding on people since the cross, I did have to learn not to go to the extreme of disregarding it altogether. It still contains many timeless truths and principles which are there for our benefit, as well as providing the grim background of humanity's history—failures we should learn from, along with good examples. See 1 Corinthians 10:6,11; Romans 15:4; 2 Peter 1:19-21 and 2 Timothy 3:15-17.

Gifts of the Holy Spirit

I said a bit about this, and I've written plenty about it elsewhere, but since you asked…

A good place to start on this is Hebrews 2:4, as it is the only place in scripture where the term "gifts of the Holy Spirit" is used. If I'd paid attention to this verse from the start, I would have saved myself a lot of time and trouble with this topic. I can't blame the looseness of the translation I was using at the time, as it spells out what the verbs and participles indicate in the Greek: "At the same time God added his witness to theirs by performing all kinds of miracles and wonders and by distributing the gifts of the Holy Spirit according to his will."

The passage tells us *when* God was testifying "by signs and wonders and various miracles and by gifts of the Holy Spirit", and *with whom* he was testifying. When was he doing it? When the message of salvation was being confirmed by those who heard the Lord announce it (men known as apostles of Christ). *With whom* was God testifying? Those very same apostles (which reminds me of what Mark 16:20 says). So here in Hebrews 2:4 we are told the timeframe in which God gave gifts of the Holy Spirit: during the apostolic era.

Acts 8 is a great place to learn why the gifts of the Spirit were limited to that era. Miracles are happening to and through Philip the evangelist, and in verses 14-19 we see that Philip could not pass that ability onto anyone else. That was for the apostles to do. Verse 18 gives us the most direct statement in the entire New Testament about how the Holy Spirit was given: "the Spirit was given through the laying on of the apostles' hands". It took me a while to realise that this passage, with others like Acts 19:5-6, point to the era of gifts of the Spirit being limited to the apostles' generation. Of course, I'm most grateful to God for patiently bringing me to this realisation, but I'm also thankful to Jeff for pointing me in the right direction back when I still believed otherwise.

When I look at it now, I realise there isn't a passage in scripture which suggests that gifts of the Holy Spirit would last till the end of the world. Why didn't I notice that from the start? One reason must surely be that I didn't think to even consider this question. I've learned that we must always ask this question when reading scripture: To whom did this originally apply, and does scripture indicate that it also applies to me?

Obedience

I told you about how I came to realise the importance of obedience to God. What I also learned with the help of the Pollocks and Jackmans was that obedience comes down to "Do as I say". I know this sounds like stating the obvious, and I did in fact learn this from my parents. But I had been taught, in religious circles, a much looser concept of obedience. Let's see if I can explain this.

When my mother sent me up the street to buy a loaf of white bread and a carton of milk, I knew from a very young age that she didn't have to tell me, "Don't buy any lollies, or Passiona." I was to simply do as I was told. When my father sent me to the shed to get a hammer, I knew that's all I was to get. I wasn't to bring the rasp and the saw as well. He didn't have to tell me not to get the saw or the rasp or drill. If I brought the axe, my father would quite rightly (and severely, I'd tip) question what I thought I was doing. If I said, "Oh, well, the butt end of the axe can do the job. What's the big difference?" he would quite directly say, "The difference is **I said**…"

This is what we read about obedience in the scriptures. For example, God commanded Noah to build a container ("ark") out of gopher wood. He didn't have to say, "Thou shalt not use pine or myrtle, nor shalt thou use oak or red gum or mountain ash." Noah just did as he was told. He didn't throw in a few planks of myrtle when it suited him. In the words of Genesis 6:22, "Noah did this; he did all that God commanded him." (ESV) That's obedience: just do it. In the words of Deuteronomy 12:32, "Everything that I command you, you shall be careful to do. You shall not add to it or take from it." (ESV)

This is why there are cases of people being punished for doing something other than what God commanded. When God says, "Do this", it goes without saying that he doesn't want us to do anything but that. Don't add to it; don't take away from it. So we read of two priests who took their censers and "put fire in them and placed incense on it; then they presented before Yahweh illegitimate fire, which he had not commanded them. So fire went out from before Yahweh, and it consumed them so that they died before Yahweh" (Lev 10:1-2 LEB). That's what they are remembered for. "But Nadab and Abihu died when they offered unauthorised fire before the LORD" (Num 26:61 ESV). All they did was use fire which God had not commanded. All they did was disobey God.

It's cases like that, along with King Saul's, that brought home to me that when God commands something of us, he expects us to stick with it. Obedience isn't doing as much as we agree with, or adding extra ("unauthorised") bits to suit our tastes. Obedience is just doing it. It's a very consistent lesson all the way through the Bible, and of course Jesus said if we love him, obedience will flow from that love (Jn 14:15).

Instrumental Music

When you grow up with something, you think it's normal. I had no idea that instrumental music was not a part of ordinary church experience for most of the 2000 years since Christ. Its widespread use in churches is a comparatively recent historical development. The reason it was absent to start with is quite simple: the apostles simply did not teach disciples to use instruments when singing encouragement to one another or praise to God; so in obedience, Christians didn't use musical instruments to worship God. Doing so would be tantamount to "offering unauthorised fire".

It took me a while to get used to this. I accepted it, but getting used to it is a different thing, and living in modern day Australia brought some tricky questions on how I should apply this. For example, what about the praise songs I had written which relied so heavily on instrumental accompaniment? And what about the records I owned which had religious music on them? Should I listen to them, or get rid of them? Later, when I was on community radio, were those songs ruled out from broadcasting? What about when I played piano for my own enjoyment: should I keep away from all those tunes which are from religious songs? The answer seems quite simple to me now, having resolved it in my own mind. I'll tell you how I have nutted it out, but I'm sure that some will have resolved it differently to me. "Each one must be fully convinced in his own mind."

When God tells us to sing praises to him (e.g. James 5:19), we just do it. When he commands us to teach and admonish one another with psalms, hymns and spiritual songs (Col 3:16), we should just do that, too. Don't add to it or subtract from it. But those instructions don't say anything about what records to play on the radio, what songs to listen to on your iPod, or what songs to perform as entertainment at a concert. Passages like Philippians 4:8 and Ephesians 4:29 are more relevant in those circumstances.

The outcome of this realisation is that, if I hear a song—whether on a recording or live—addressed to God but offered up in a way that amounts to "unauthorised fire", then I know it doesn't pass the Philippians 4:8 test. I know how displeasing "unauthorised fire" is to God, so I take no pleasure in hearing it; it does not edify or even entertain me. However, when I hear a song that acknowledges truth, but is not addressing God, surely that passes the Philippians 4:8 and Ephesians 4:29 test. For example, the song may say that God is good, or that "Man Gave Names to All the Animals"[61], or "He's Got the Whole World in His Hands". There's certainly nothing wrong with speaking the truth in song and, if it's not being offered as "unauthorised fire" (so to speak), it's much better than a lot of the music I could listen to as I drive to work or weed the garden.

But then there are songs with lyrics addressing God, which are performed purely for entertainment and do not purport to worship God. An example which comes to mind is *Fire and Rain* by James Taylor, where he says, "Won't you look down upon me, Jesus; you gotta help me make a stand. You just got to see me through another day."[62] That song acknowledges his need for Jesus, but James Taylor is performing that song for our entertainment. It's not offered as an act of worship to Jesus. Likewise, we understand that, when Jack Johnson performs *Sitting, Waiting, Wishing*, the "you" in the lyrics isn't addressed to the audience, and whoever was the "you" in the song is not present to have it addressed to her. "Please ignore the next few lines, 'cause they're directed at you"[63] is simply performed to the audience, not directed at them. So even though the lyrics are addressed to a particular person, the song is not being sung to them on the recording or at the concert. It's being sung to the listeners, the audience. The same is true of some songs which refer to or address God, but are not offered to him as worship. Ephesians 5:19, Colossians 3:16, James 5:13b and 1 Corinthians 14:15,26 are not talking about such cases, so I don't apply those passages where they don't apply.

Calling on the Name of the Lord

Romans 10:13 contains a statement I saw and heard quoted often: "Whoever calls on the name of the Lord shall be saved" (NKJV). It's a quote from Joel 2, and is also quoted in Acts 2:21. The trouble was, people seemed to speak of "calling on the name of the Lord" to mean what they wanted it to mean, so quoting it was really achieving nothing when discussing what a person had to do to be saved.

---

[61] *Animals (Man Gave Names To All The Animals)*, Bob Dylan. ©1979 Special Rider Music.

[62] *Fire and Rain*, James Taylor. ©1970 EMI Blackwood Music Inc., Country Road Music, Randy Scruggs Music, Warner-Tamerlane Publishing Corp.

[63] *Sitting, Waiting, Wishing*, Jack Hody Johnson ©2005 Bubble Toes Publishing.

In those two passages, my golden Good News Bible, rather than translating it, paraphrased it like this: "Everyone who calls out to the Lord for help will be saved." As paraphrases go, that's not too bad. It gets across the idea that you're appealing to God for help, pretty much as Peter did in Matthew 14:30 when he began to sink — "Lord, save me!" But in Acts 22:16, where Saul is exhorted, "Arise and be baptised, and wash away your sins, calling on the name of the Lord", that same Bible of mine paraphrased it quite differently. It said, "Get up and be baptized and have your sins washed away by praying to him." That's quite a different paraphrase to those other verses; it radically changes the meaning of Acts 22:16. Why did they do that?

What the verse actually says (if you're using a reliable translation) helped me understand how I could call on the name of the Lord. Being baptised, having my sins washed away, was an act of calling on the name of the Lord. That's what the verse clearly expresses. As 1 Peter 3:21 says, baptism is "an appeal to God for a good conscience": in coming to Jesus for cleansing, we're in effect calling out "Lord, save me!" We're calling on his name.

What I didn't grasp at the time was that we must continue to call on the name of the Lord after we're baptised. We still need his ongoing cleansing for the rest of our lives, so Paul in 1 Corinthians 1:2 speaks of God's people as "those who in every place are calling on the name of Jesus Christ our Lord". As we continue serving Christ, we depend upon his cleansing to keep us alive spiritually (1 John 1:7).

The Hope of Glory: Christ in You, and You in Christ

Another thing I didn't have my head around during my years before my baptism was the concept of being "in Christ". I certainly knew the term "in Christ". We even sang about it: one favourite old hymn was "In Christ There is No East or West".

The Bible speaks of a people who are in Christ, and have Christ in them. Looking for a biblical church as I was, I should have been looking for people who are *in Christ* and who have *Christ in them*. If you don't have a clear idea of what you're looking for, how are you going to know you've found it? How do you spot them? I found seeing Christ in people easier than seeing people who are in Christ. I think I'll have to explain that.

I see Christ in people when I see Christ's traits in them. They are giving people, who have a peace and joy about them, who glow with that inner beauty that they have learned from Jesus. It's easiest to see that in people when they have it in large degree. But the outstanding characteristic of Jesus was his devotion to doing God's will. He wasn't just a really nice person with a good head on his shoulders. He was devoted to God, in full submission to his will. For example:

> My Father, if it is possible, let this cup pass from me; nevertheless, not as I will, but as you will . . . My Father, if this cup cannot pass away from me unless I drink it, let your will be done.　　*Matthew 26:39,42*

> I do not seek my own will but the will of the Father who sent me.
> *John 5:30*

> He humbled himself by becoming obedient to the point of death.
> *Philippians 2:8*

So that's what we will see in those who imitate Christ, who have Christ living in them:

> Not everyone who says to me, 'Lord, Lord,' will enter the kingdom of heaven, but he who does the will of my Father who is in heaven.
> *Matthew 7:21*

> For whoever does the will of my Father in heaven, he is my brother and sister and mother.　　*Matthew 12:50*

I've met a lot of people who show many Christlike traits, but who lack this crucial characteristic. But when I walked into the Pollocks' house at 17 years of age, I met people who truly had Christ in them. They weren't perfect, but they were the genuine article.

Telling if someone is *in Christ* is not so easy, because you have to get to know what they believe, and whether they have actually made the transition into Christ. When the Pollocks first met me, they didn't know whether I was in the Lord. They had to get to know me. It wouldn't have taken long for them to see whether Christ was in my life, but a lot of people have Christ in their lives; they just haven't gotten into Christ. When Christ came into the lives of people when he walked the earth, he made a difference. Some couldn't stand him in their lives, even to the point of wanting him dead. Others exulted in the blessings of having Jesus in their lives.

Not only was this true when Jesus walked the earth, but also after he had returned to heaven. From Acts 7:58, we read that Jesus was in the life of a young Pharisee named Saul. Saul gave a lot of time to Jesus—that is, he gave a lot of time to trying to stamp out his followers. His attacks on disciples of Christ were in fact attacks on Jesus himself, as the Lord later pointed out (Acts 9:4-5). Clearly, well before his conversion to Christ, Saul had Jesus in his life. And just before he got to Damascus, Saul had an amazing encounter with Christ. The Lord came into his life in a dramatic way which had a powerful impact on Saul; but even then Saul did not get into Christ till three days after that, at the urging of Ananias (Acts 22:16).

I knew that all spiritual blessings are in Christ. Ephesians 1 says that plainly, as well as mentioning a range of specific blessings in him—things like redemption, forgiveness of sins through his blood, and an inheritance in heaven by his grace. Elsewhere we read of other wonderful blessings. But what I had not noticed was that there were only two verses which spoke of how we get "into Christ": Romans 6:3 and Galatians 3:27. They tell us the one thing which gets us "into Christ": baptism in the name of Jesus. This is why, in my account, I speak of being "baptised into Christ".

Getting into Christ is crucial to our spiritual well-being. If Satan can stop souls getting into Christ, he succeeds in keeping them from all of those spiritual blessings which are in Christ. It's obvious that this is exactly what he has been up to. But he can't pull the wool over everyone's eyes. As God has promised, "seek and you will find"; he rewards those who diligently seek him (Matthew 7:7; Hebrews 11:6).

But getting into Christ isn't the end. As Roy Griffin said to me all those years ago, it's the beginning. Many more years before that, Paul wrote (in Galatians 4:19) that we must go on to have Christ formed in us. It's a growth process, and I am still on that path of growth towards Christlikeness. The journey continues! There's many ways this is explained in scripture, but in Galatians 2:20 Paul sums up the life which is lived in Christ, with Christ living in us. It begins with our being crucified with Christ (as per Romans 6:3-5), and goes on from there. "The life which I now live in the flesh I live by the faith of the Son of God." Once we're in Christ, we must have Christ in us. That, says Paul in Colossians 1:27, is the hope of glory.

The End

Sometimes I wonder why we give so much attention to what's going to happen in the future, rather than giving more attention to what the Lord calls us to do in the present.

Those books I had read about events soon to come to pass failed the test of prophecy given in Deuteronomy 18:21-22. What they predicted did not come to pass when they said it would. Of course, most of the writers weren't claiming to be prophets. Sure, David Wilkerson claimed to have received a vision, so that's a claim to prophecy, but Lindsay and Deyo were just interpreting the scriptures. It's clear, however, that time has proved them all wrong, just as it proved others wrong in preceding generations, such as Ellen

G White, Charles Taze Russell, Joseph Smith, and those who said Hitler was the Beast of Revelation, to be followed by Christ's return soon afterwards.

In all those eras, there were others who took a different interpretation of scripture, disciples who saw in scripture a different picture of what would precede the end of the world. They saw the Bible saying that Christ would return at a time not anticipated by people. That's what I began to see in scriptures too, with the help of those teaching me in my spiritual infancy.

In contrast to what Jesus said in Matthew 24:1-34 about his action against Jerusalem in that generation, where he emphasised that his audience would see signs to know that the time was near, he went on to say that his final return would not be like that. It would be a day and hour when he is not expected. In Matthew 25:1-13 he likened the time of his return to a bridegroom, delayed for the feast, coming when some who were awaiting his return were not prepared.

He also said that it will be like it was in the days of Noah: people would be eating and drinking, marrying and giving in marriage. That sounds like life will be going on without any significant crisis. The other grim feature of Noah's day was that godlessness and iniquity had increased to the point that hardly anyone was found who cared about pleasing and honouring God. When I think how God called it quits with the ancient world of that day, I am reminded of the parallel 2 Peter 3:5-7 draws, where Peter compares the destruction of Noah's day to the final destruction of the world. The question Jesus asked, "When the Son of Man comes, will he find faith on earth?" does not engender optimism about the state of humanity when Jesus returns. It sounds like it will be down to a handful, as in Noah's day.

Writing to the Thessalonian church about the end of the world, Paul says in 1 Thessalonians 5 that, just when people are saying "peace and safety", then sudden destruction would hit them. So the "all is well—steady as she goes" attitude is foretold to be a characteristic of the time just before the end. It certainly doesn't sound like tribulation, plague, water turned to blood, and everyone gnawing their tongues in pain from their afflictions.

Paul also, even in the first century, described the whole of creation as groaning and awaiting release from its bondage to decay (Romans 8:19-22). We live in a decaying world, and the older and more run-down the place becomes, the more we should be reminded that it is destined to perish—to melt with fervent heat (2 Peter 3:7,10-12). Henny Pennies run around in a panic about the state of the planet, when humankind should realise that the Creator has already told us to expect its demise. It is only a temporary habitat, destined for destruction when Christ returns. It's the state of humankind that should concern us most.

Scripture is full of prophetic predictions. I've noticed that it's common for people to take many such prophecies and say they are being fulfilled (or soon will be) today, when actually the prophecy was fulfilled centuries ago. Matthew 24:4-34 is a classic example, but the latest case which comes to mind is Isaiah's prediction about the destruction of Damascus. There was a flurry of claims in 2013 that this was being fulfilled in the Syrian civil war, when we can easily ascertain that Isaiah's prediction was fulfilled hundreds of years Before Christ. I've learned that, before we go believing claims that some ancient prophecy is talking about events in our day, we should look carefully at what the prophet says he was talking about, and look into whether it has been fulfilled already.

Scripture tells us how the world is going to end, and who is going to end it, so doomsday claims don't panic me. From what scripture tells us, I get a picture of where the course of human history is headed, with the very end something to look forward to, rather than fear, if we're in Christ. As the world continues to move further away from God and deeper into defiant rebellion against him, the tide against the people of God will of course become stronger and stronger. So I don't expect an easy ride ahead, or a flood of converts in the future; just a few, as those who are recognisable as followers of Christ become a remnant harder and harder to find. I really do wonder: when the Son of Man comes, will he find faith on the earth?

Maranatha!
("Come, Lord!")

Sources Referred to in This Book

Flew, Anthony and Varghese, Roy Abraham. *There Is a God: How the
World's Most Notorious Atheist Changed His Mind*
Harper Collins, New York, 2007.

Gish, Duane T. *Evolution? The Fossils Say No!*
Creation-Life Publishers, San Diego, 1979.

Milne, A A. *When We Were Very Young*,
Methuen & Co., London, 1924.

The Macquarie Dictionary, Macquarie Library, McMahons Point, 1981.

Cates, Mickey *Baptism* [Song]
©1999 Sony/ATV Cross Keys Publishing.
When this book was published the lyrics were available at
http://genius.com/Kenny-chesney-baptism-lyrics

Bible translations cited or quoted

EMTV – English Majority Text Version of the Holy Bible, New Testament.
©2002-2003 Paul W. Esposito.

ESV – The Holy Bible, English Standard Version
©2002 Collins, part of Harper Collins Publishers.

LEB – Lexham English Bible ©2010, 2012 Logos Bible Software

NASB – New American Standard Bible
Thomas Nelson Publishers, Nashville, 1977

NIV – New International Version ©1978 New York International Bible
Society

NKJV – The Holy Bible, New King James Version
Thomas Nelson Publishers, Nashville, 1994.

TEV – Good News Bible ~ Today's English Version
American Bible Society, New York, 1976